For years I've hoped for some real research about how and why groups work. Yours feels the most accessible. I'm not being polite when I say this, but if a person was only going to buy one book on small groups, I'd direct them to yours!

Bill Search, pastor and author of
Essential Guide for Small Group Leaders

This book speaks visionary truth with empowering grace. Combining fascinating real-life research with insightful questions, thoughtful analysis, compelling models, and pragmatic recommendations, this is a unique and valuable resource for small group leaders and ministries.

Carolyn Taketa, small groups pastor and
host of the *GroupTalk* podcast

Small group ministries are the great conundrum in most American churches. Everybody says they're vital, but few have figured out how to make them actually work. Frankly, we've been given too much theory and idealism and not enough research highlighting the best practices that really work. This book will be a great help to the church at large.

Larry Osborne, pastor at North Coast
Church, and author of *Sticky Church*

Based on rock-solid research, this gem unearths the strengths and weaknesses of many small group ministries, and offers assessment tools to evaluate your ministry. But, most of all, this is a leadership book. When leaders read and apply *Leading Small Groups That Thrive*, they'll grow into effective, confident, transformational disciple-makers.

Rick Howerton, small groups expert, author,
and church planter at The Bridge Church.

The staggering amount of research in this book has been used to create practical, doable takeaways for anyone in small group leadership who wants to see the people in their groups thrive. I'm SO thankful this book is now available to leaders.

Amy Jackson, director of The Perch and
former publisher of SmallGroups.com

Want to learn the secrets of sustainable momentum to overcome groups that struggle, limp along, and eventually sputter out? This outstanding book is chock full of fresh insights, practical tools, and a powerful roadmap that can lead any group to the next level. If you've ever wondered how to cast a compelling vision for small group life that equips existing leaders and raises up new ones, this is a must-read! I can't wait to get this into the hands of our leaders!

Tim Lucas, lead pastor of Liquid Church

We're constantly asked: How can I improve my small groups ministry? I'm grateful for this book that provides great answers to the questions small group leaders consistently ask. Based on robust research and the science behind what makes groups work, this book lays out an actionable plan to take your group from barely surviving to thriving. It's my pleasure to recommend it to you.

Steve Gladen, pastor of small groups at Saddleback Church and author of *Planning Small Groups with Purpose*

Since the church was born, small groups have always been a vital part of Christianity, and they will only become more important in the future. This book is a gift to God's family, filled with resources to give you the right foundation and practice for thriving small groups.

David Guzik, author and Bible commentator, *Enduring Word*

Leading Small Groups That Thrive is an important book for all of us who realize that the church is not an event, but a community with a cause! Ryan, Courtney, and Jason combine passion for small groups with solid research, real-life stories and practical tools to show us how to get good at groups. If you want to know how to make disciples and foster genuine Biblical community then this is a must read!

Dave Ferguson, pastor, lead visionary for NewThing, and author of *Hero Maker*

This fresh, powerful book is gold. Both engaging and informative, it shows small groups that thrive and empowers leaders to move their groups to greater health. Seasoned leaders will be surprised by the new insights that the book brings out.

Warren Bird, coauthor of 32 books for church leaders, and Michelle C. Bird, small groups leader and trainer

Inspirational. Catalytic. Strategic. Read this book to discover key questions, powerful mindset shifts, and essential leader habits for a flourishing small groups ministry.

D. Scott Barfoot, PhD, Dallas Theological Seminary

RYAN T. HARTWIG
COURTNEY W. DAVIS
JASON A. SNIFF

LEADING
(SMALL
GROUPS)
THAT
THRIVE

FIVE SHIFTS TO TAKE YOUR SMALL
GROUP TO THE NEXT LEVEL

ZONDERVAN
REFLECTIVE

ZONDERVAN REFLECTIVE

Leading Small Groups That Thrive

Copyright © 2020 by Ryan T. Hartwig, Courtney W. Davis, and Jason A. Sniff

Requests for information should be addressed to:
Zondervan, 3900 Sparks Dr. SE, Grand Rapids, Michigan 49546

Zondervan titles may be purchased in bulk for educational, business, fundraising, or sales promotional use. For information, please email SpecialMarkets@Zondervan.com.

ISBN 978-0-310-10670-8 (softcover)
ISBN 978-0-310-12006-3 (audio)
ISBN 978-0-310-10671-5 (ebook)

Cover design: Brian Bobel Design
Cover art: Wanwi17 / istockphoto
Interior design: Denise Froehlich

Printed in the United States of America

20 21 22 23 24 / LSC / 10 9 8 7 6 5 4 3 2 1

To Gus and the guys, for 20+ years
of friendship and discipleship.
RTH

To Matt, Luke, and Theo, my favorite
and most formative small group.
CWD

To Nicole and Team Sniff, Jim Probst for taking
a chance on me, and my amazing team.
JAS

CONTENTS

PART 3: THREE ESSENTIAL DISCIPLINES TO SUSTAIN YOUR LONG-TERM EFFECTIVENESS

FOREWORD

Every soul has a story. And they all involve a community. Or the lack of one.

That's why I've given my life to small group disciple-making. I imagine that's also why you've picked up this book. We know that there's no significant transformation in one person without another.

The same goes for the souls leading small groups ministries: we need each other. As we lead others in transformational communities, we need to be sharpened by a community of fellow leaders with the same mission and passion.

I believe you will find such fellow leaders in Courtney, Jason, and Ryan. As soon as you read their stories in the opening, you'll know that you are sitting with small groups *champions*. Not merely gurus.

They prove it by doing something rather remarkable for a book like this, though it should probably be how more of these things are written: they invite even more friends along for the community conversation that is *Leading Small Groups That Thrive*.

Alongside the authors' deft balance of research and real life, you will hear from a diverse community of leaders in the small groups world at the end of each chapter. Each brings nuance and frontline consideration to the material. Some of them are known friends and mentors, and others you will meet for the first time.

This is a book about community written in community. It's a community that helps me, and I've led small groups for almost twenty years now. That's long enough to learn a few things, and long enough to build up some pride against learning new things or relearning some fundamentals. The community that wrote this book reminds me that there are new lessons in old truths about small groups ministry. They've researched the essentials, and they share what they've found here.

Sometimes it is surprising. The stats and numbers might upend some long-held assumptions that I . . . you . . . we have about small groups ministry (What do you mean that twelve isn't the perfect number for a small group?), but you'll find the research undeniable. You might find your course being gently corrected. I did.

How many times will I have to be reminded that leaders are our lifeblood in small groups ministry? Thank you, Lord, for Courtney, Jason, Ryan, and Co. for showing me why all over again!

They helped remind me that small group disciple-making is not limited by a building, space, or financial issues. Never will be. Groups are only ever limited by lack of leaders, their health, and investment. Leading a small groups ministry is dependent on leading through others. That's classic Ephesians 4 ministry. Groups should be the crown jewel of discovering, developing, and deploying leaders in our local churches. The community of writers here helped me refine some of our own plans for fresh investment in leader development in our groups ministry at The Village Church.

And this book lays out an actionable roadmap for leaders to recruit, shape, and build groups that lead others into life transformation. This is the development tool that leaders need.

If you can't tell by now, let me tell it plain: I got excited about small groups all over again as I read this book! That's why you should read it. And share it.

If you're a pastor, use the work here to help your own community of local church leaders "get" small groups even more. We small groups people tend to be an intuitive bunch. And we don't always grasp why our lead pastor, or elders, or executive team don't seem to love (or understand) groups as much as we do. This book is a practical help to you. The community of writers here has given us the gift of fresh metrics and data to cultivate better strategy and operations for small groups ministry in our context. Consider using some of this gold next time you share with your own group leaders or executive pastor. Share it over a series of training sessions with your leaders. I've already started.

Groups ministry will always be more art than science. It's messy that way. Courtney, Jason, Ryan, and friends give us a blend of art and science here that will help small group leaders better participate in the mission of God in their living rooms week after week.

I'm so grateful for this book and the kindred spirits who authored it. They've helped me in my art, adding increased color and perspective to the craft of cultivating small groups that thrive.

Jared Steven Musgrove, DMin.
Groups pastor, The Village Church
Cofounder & executive director, communityleadership.org

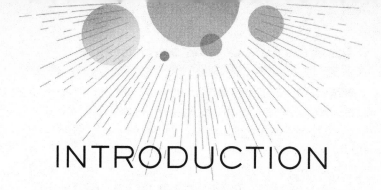

INTRODUCTION

Why We Needed This Book
(and Why You Might Also)

RYAN'S STORY

It all started in August 1997. I was a sophomore in college. At the student leadership retreat before the start of school, I was eating lunch with five of my buddies when Gus, our campus pastor, came up to our table and uttered the words that would begin a twenty-plus-year journey of discipleship and friendship.

"Hey guys, I see something in you. *Can I disciple you this year?*"

We were flattered. A few of us had just attended his discipleship workshop. Now Gus wanted to disciple us? A few weeks later, we began meeting together, first studying the book of Philippians in his office, and then interspersing many rounds of frisbee golf with serious conversation and Bible study. The following year, we met weekly, and Gus got each of us involved in bringing the Word—so he could not only give each of us the opportunity to teach, but coach us as we did. The following year, Gus made it clear that he expected each of us to find a group of guys we could invest in and disciple, too. We did, but we kept meeting together as well, becoming the best of friends along the way. When graduation arrived, we committed to getting together once a year for the rest of our lives.

Last May, we celebrated twenty-three years together. We've laughed, cried, and yelled together. We've lived lots of life together. We've seen God do incredible things. God has spoken to me through these friends, and through me, he has spoken to them. I've shared some of the greatest experiences of my life with these guys.

Perhaps our most poignant moment together happened during our annual trip a few years ago. Late one night, God wooed back to himself one of my friends who had wandered away from faith—and he used us in that process as we prayed for and with our friend, battled the enemy's lies together, and cheered as Jesus revealed himself to my friend just as the sun came up the next morning! This was our twenty-first-century version of the story of the paralytic's friends digging through the roof and lowering their sick friend to Jesus, which is recounted in Mark 2. It was amazing!

But it hasn't always been that way. Together we've fought, wrestled, and almost given up more than a few times. But God has used this group of men to help each of us look a little bit more like Jesus as the years have passed.

When we first got together, Gus made it clear that this group wasn't just for us. It was something for us to share with others. Since then, I've led multiple groups of college students and young men trying to make their way in the world. My wife and I have also led groups of families seeking community and growth, as well as young married couples desiring to serve God in their marriages, careers, and families. We've made great friends, we've seen God move in amazing ways, and we are all better for those experiences.

I believe in groups with everything in me, but if I'm honest, the groups I've led along the way have struggled for some of the same reasons your groups likely have: lack of commitment, fear of breaking up (for the sake of the gospel), confused purpose, dominating or nearly nonexistent members. I've never felt like I had all the answers to the challenges that have arisen, but I want those answers for myself, and for you, so that all of us can lead groups that thrive. That's why I've engaged this project and why I'm writing this book.

JASON'S STORY

Over forty years ago, my mom and dad were living in Rockford, Illinois. They were invited to join a group of people who met in a home to spend time together and study the Bible. My parents wanted relationships with other Christians, but they were reluctant to commit since they had never been part of a small group before. They said yes anyway.

What ensued was a group of couples and families who committed to living in community and who challenged each other to grow in Jesus. Through group and individual discipleship, my parents experienced the power of like-minded friends who truly cared for each other. My parents came from family backgrounds riddled with divorce and addiction, and in their small group they encountered new models for their marriage and family.

When I was a year old, my parents, through the loving support and guidance of their small group, decided to give their lives to Jesus and to raise my brother and me to love Jesus and serve him. Their time in that small group changed the trajectory of their lives and provided new purpose and direction.

Years later, when my wife and I moved to Normal, Illinois, we faced a similar situation. We needed a new church family—and a group of people we could call our own. We struggled for a while to find a church and community that seemed right. Several months later, a friend invited my wife to Thanksgiving dinner with her small group. Three years later, I was hired to help our church's small groups ministry grow.

I still chuckle every time I think about my parents' journey and how it reveals God's sense of humor and providence. Small groups continue to deeply impact my own family journey. My family, "Team Sniff," now includes six kids (a small group in and of itself!), and I have been on staff for over nine years as a small groups pastor charged with helping others connect into groups and helping leaders and groups be the best they can be.

One seemingly innocuous invitation to visit a gathering of people forty-some years ago has transformed my entire family's journey. If done well, I think such groups can transform you and yours.

COURTNEY'S STORY

I was invited by sorority sisters. Every week, eight to ten girls gathered in the USC Theta house for a Bible study. They were friends of mine, but I wasn't yet a Christian. It was because of this group of smart, ambitious, kind, fun young women that I started to understand who Jesus was and what community was for.

I graduated from the University of Southern California a year and a half later, found a church, and plugged in. Unfortunately, the small group of young professional women I joined at that church had the makings of a reality TV show—drama, gossip, doubts about God and the church, and a lack of direction. At one point, the church leaders had to intervene to make an attempt at reconciliation. It didn't work. Nope. No more church small groups for me.

I was on a skiing and snowboarding trip with a sorority sister when I met Lisa. We got to know one another well on the road and on our snowboards. When we came down from the mountain, the three of us committed to lean into our desire for community and hospitality, starting what would become our Sunday Supper Club. We'd meet for dinner and play games with young professional Christians. Sometimes it was just fun; other times we went deep. It was the first time I experienced Christian community as an adult.

Years later, my husband Matt and I were both volunteering as leaders in the high school ministry at our church in Santa Barbara. We hosted small groups of high school students and the college-age high school leaders. We may not have been perfectly fit to lead, but we were willing. I participated in Beth Moore Bible studies, Matt attended men's prayer breakfasts, and after we had our first kiddo, we participated in home groups with the parents of our former high schoolers. To be in relationship with those parents was such a joy for all of us—they weren't old enough to be our parents, and we weren't young enough to be their kids. They spoke such encouragement to us and prayed bold prayers with and for us during a season of great change.

Now, Matt and I co-lead a church growth group of young professionals in their mid-to late twenties, equipping them with the Word of God to send them back out into their workplaces and relationships more sure of God's purposeful placement and plan. Again, we aren't always convinced we're fit to lead, but we are still willing.

While I was ready to write off groups forever after that first church small group disaster, fifteen years later, I'm convinced that the Lord can do incredible things through regular, intimate gatherings of broken, hopeful people. But I've wondered for years how to participate with God in facilitating the incredible things that can happen through groups. In my more prideful moments, I knew exactly what to do and how to do it, but in my more humble moments, I realized I still have a lot of questions.

• • •

A DIFFERENT KIND OF SMALL GROUPS BOOK

Our lives have been deeply impacted by small groups in so many different ways. The three of us want more people to be as deeply influenced in and through groups as we have been. But we've also been in your shoes, leading groups week in and week out. We've encountered difficult conversations, waning attendance and commitment, and a lack of resources to help us address our group's issues. So, when we—two social scientists and a small groups pastor—started talking, we decided to ask good questions that would result in better answers to the most vexing challenges group leaders face.

The perspective we've taken is unique from any other book on small groups. We've integrated church-based research on small groups (hearing from over 800 small group members, not just leaders), in-depth academic knowledge of small group and team communication, practical examples based on visits we made to numerous small groups, and our own experiences leading small groups and small groups programs over decades.

Leading Small Groups That Thrive provides a research-driven yet practical resource that group leaders can use immediately.

Leading Small Groups That Thrive provides a research-driven yet practical resource that group leaders can use immediately.

OUR RESEARCH ON MEMBERS, LEADERS, AND PASTORS

The truth is that many small groups in churches, colleges, universities, and communities like yours are thriving. So we found those groups and studied them. Our major research project ran from 2017–2019, during which we worked with smallgroups.com, who helped us collect survey data from small groups pastors, small group leaders, and small group members. This yielded data from almost 100 pastors, over 150 small group leaders, and over 800 small group members, representing over 100 of the healthiest small groups from those churches, which included both mainline and evangelical churches. In addition, we visited many small groups and watched them in action. We conducted dozens of interviews with group members, leaders, and small groups pastors to learn what is working, what is not, and what resources they need to be fully equipped for the long haul.

Most studies on small groups take their cues from just leaders or just pastors. Very few actually include the voices of group members. Small group members told us about their leaders, their church's small group priorities, and their personal engagement and spiritual growth. By listening to group members talk about their groups and what makes them great, we've gleaned insights to help you make great choices about how to lead your group and maximize your group's impact. Hearing directly from group members enabled us to learn how groups *actually* contribute to their members' spiritual growth. While groups composed of spiritually mature Christians may look like effective groups, their effectiveness may be attributed primarily to the spiritual maturity of individuals rather than the groups themselves.

Hearing directly from group members enabled us to learn how groups *actually* contribute to their members' spiritual growth.

We were most interested in identifying *group* practices that contribute to growth in *individual members'* spiritual health.

You might be asking how we measured spiritual health. Good question. There are probably as many ways to slice and dice spiritual maturity as there are churches, but we didn't want to create a new scorecard. So we adapted the five areas of spiritual health that Steve Gladen proposed in his book *Small Groups with Purpose*[1] and uses in his own ministry at Saddleback Church. The five areas include: worship, fellowship, discipleship, ministry, and evangelism. We used Gladen's established elements of spiritual health to investigate how much each member's small group contributed to these specific areas of his or her individual spiritual health—and to learn the factors that most influenced growth through groups.[2] We also included assimilation, defined as the extent to which one feels connected to and a part of the larger church body, as small group membership is often related to feelings of belonging to a church.

Our study revealed many interesting—and, in some cases, unexpected—findings. For instance, we found:

- The more time a group spends in prayer, the less a group contributes to its members' spiritual growth. In contrast, the more time the leader spends in prayer, the more the group contributes to spiritual growth. We're not suggesting that praying should be exclusively limited to group leaders, but this finding truly demonstrates that the impact of a praying leader cannot be underestimated.
- The more time a group worships together and talks through logistics and announcements, the more it contributes to its members' spiritual growth. Those must be some amazing, powerful announcements!
- Groups that place less emphasis on discipleship see more spiritual growth among their members. How can that be?
- The most effective groups were either really small (fewer than eight members) or pretty big (more than seventeen members). However, the majority of the groups in our sample were

composed of ten to twelve people. That means the group size many have always thought is optimal is actually not optimal for spurring spiritual growth.

- Newer groups that had been meeting for less than three months contributed the most to individual spiritual growth. As the length of time the group had been together increased, the group's contribution to individual spiritual growth decreased over time (except in the unlikely event that the group stayed together for more than eleven years). On the other hand, we discovered that outstanding group practices can counteract the decline in impact that occurs as groups age.

In many cases, our data suggested conclusions that go against the grain of much of the common-sense advice out there. Of course, not all of our findings were so scandalous. Our data also affirmed many things that won't surprise you. We found that a leader's commitment to their group makes a huge difference. So does the amount of time a group spends together during its weekly meetings (more is better). And groups that report high-quality discussions and are willing to engage conflict constructively cultivate rich soil for the spiritual growth of their members.

We unpack findings like these throughout the book.

To all we learned through our study, we also add our years of experience leading and participating in numerous small groups, and leading and consulting with small groups ministries, churches, and ministry organizations. Through this project, we've combined rigorous social science methodology, expert statistical analysis, and in-depth knowledge of the science of team and group communication to provide you with practical, relevant tips and methods to guide you in leading thriving small groups. You are not just reading what three people think about small groups. Instead, you are learning from hundreds of people and their experiences, all condensed and communicated in a way that tells you what the research says, why it matters, and how to apply it.

WHAT TO EXPECT IN THE
PAGES THAT FOLLOW

In the chapters to come, we will provide you with advice and ideas backed by research that will help you avoid, or at least minimize, the challenges often experienced in groups so that you can maximize the benefits that result from thriving, transformational group experiences.

In part 1 (chapters 1–3), we pose three questions you must ask right away as you think about leading a small group that thrives. Ultimately, answering these three questions will help you develop a clear vision for your small group and a workable plan to realize that vision. Chapter 1 explores the value and power of small groups, even amidst their challenges. We offer a powerful vision for healthy and effective small groups, or, in our words, "groups that thrive." In chapter 2, we provide a picture of what great group leaders do and lay out our *Leading Small Groups That Thrive* model. Then, in chapter 3, we provide a conceptual roadmap for how groups typically grow and develop. This forms the foundation for the practices we lay out in the rest of the book.

In part 2 (chapters 4–8), we explain five necessary shifts that must occur in order for a small group to thrive, outlining what you need to do to help your group move to the next level of health and effectiveness:

1. **Confused to Compelling:** Energize Your Group by Articulating Your Purpose
2. **Disengaged to Dedicated:** Set the Stage to Keep People Coming Back
3. **Mine to Ours:** Cultivate Commitment through Shared Ownership
4. **Trivial to Transformative:** Stimulate Meaningful Discussions
5. **Avoidance to Embrace:** Engage Difficult Conversations without Destroying Your Group

We ground our discussion of these practices in our research and offer real-life examples from groups we've seen over the years. We don't stop at explaining *what* to do; we go the extra mile to teach you *how* to make the shift in your group, no matter what stage it's in.

In part 3 (chapters 9–12), we address how you can expand and sustain your influence within and beyond your group. We outline three essential disciplines to sustain your long-term effectiveness as a leader:

1. **Your Care:** Cultivating and Sustaining Your Own Health
2. **Your Legacy:** Recruiting and Raising Up New Leaders
3. **Your Charge:** Expanding and Multiplying Groups

We conclude by helping you identify next steps to spur growth in your group's effectiveness and health.

Throughout the book, we provide examples from numerous thriving small groups, Two-minute Tips to help you apply what you are reading right away, tools for individual reflection and assessment, discussion questions for use with other group leaders, and insightful contributions by expert commentators.

WHO THIS BOOK IS FOR

Whoever you are, if you want to grow as a small group leader, this book is for *you*.

Whether you're leading a group through your church, teaching a Sunday school class, facilitating table discussion at a weekly Bible study gathering, launching a micro-congregation at your local CrossFit gym, or trying to provide structure to your Thursday morning coffee group, this book is for you. If you're gathering with others with the goal of developing relationships and growing in your faith, we've written this book to help you develop your group into a healthy community that contributes to individuals' spiritual growth.

If you're new to group leadership, we'll give you a roadmap to follow to build a group that cultivates transformational moments in community. If you've been around the block a few times, we'll challenge you to rethink your strategy and offer some insights to help you better navigate the challenges you've experienced.

If you're leading a group that is struggling, we'll help you diagnose what's really wrong, then put together an action plan to spur your group toward health and effectiveness. If you're leading a group that is thriving, we'll help you understand why and help you leverage your success to expand your group's kingdom impact.

If you're a coach, consultant, trainer, or pastor who oversees small groups and shepherds leaders, this book is for you, too. While we primarily address the folks with their boots on the ground—group leaders—we'll let you eavesdrop on our conversation so you can learn how to better coach and develop leaders. We'll offer you research-based insights and a model for building thriving small groups that you can implement in your own small groups ministry. We've also included an appendix to help you identify ministry or church-wide action steps.

This is a book about next-level groups led by next-level leaders.

Whatever your vantage point, we encourage you to use this book as a thought-provoker, conversation-starter, and guide for taking your group to the next level of health and impact. This is a book about next-level groups led by next-level leaders.

Along the way, we've learned a lot about groups. Our prayer is that God would mightily use what we've learned and shared in this book to guide you, as small group leaders in churches and ministries of every size and shape and tribe, to cultivate spaces in which your members grow in Christ, individually and together, for our collective good and God's glory.

PART I

THREE QUESTIONS TO ASK RIGHT NOW

Chapter 1: What's the Big Deal about Groups?
Casting a Powerful Vision for Groups

Chapter 2: What Does a Catalytic Leader Do?
Painting a Picture of Next-Level Group Leadership

Chapter 3: How Do I Get Where I Want to Go?
Mapping a Plan to Develop a Thriving Group

Groups matter. They make a huge difference in the lives of countless people, both inside and outside the walls of the church. But too many don't. The church needs more thriving groups.

To see more thriving groups in churches and communities across our world, we need more equipped leaders who can facilitate next-level groups.

Those leaders (and the groups they lead) need good ideas and principles, and a workable plan, to drive their leadership.

CHAPTER 1

WHAT'S THE BIG DEAL ABOUT GROUPS?

Casting a Powerful Vision for Groups

Your groups matter. A lot. The reality is that the people in groups, from a research vantage point, are more likely to share their faith, repent of their sins regularly, give sacrificially, serve faithfully, and read their Bibles.[1]

—ED STETZER AND ERIC GEIGER

We know you've heard how amazing small groups are. Maybe you've even said one of these phrases:

Small groups are where community happens.
Small groups aren't one more thing to do. They are *the* thing to do.
Small groups are how we make our (big) church smaller.
Small groups *are* the church.

If you've picked up this book, you are likely invested in small groups. You've probably seen (or at least heard of) groups that thrive and succeed, and perhaps you've experienced the power of community and the growth that comes when you are connected in the body of Christ and using your gifts in ministry. Maybe you've volunteered to gather a new group or agreed to lead an existing group, and you are hoping that your group will experience life-changing community and deeper, more profound spiritual growth. Maybe you've been leading groups for a while, and you are looking to find solutions to the problems you've faced for too long.

Whatever your specific situation, you've picked up this book because you believe that groups *can* thrive, and that God can use small groups to monumentally transform individual lives, churches, and communities. This chapter outlines the realities and the potential of small groups, establishes the need for healthy small groups, and casts a vision for creating a healthy, thriving small group in your context.

SMALL GROUPS ARE HARD

Sadly, *thriving*, *transformational*, and *healthy* are not the adjectives most people would use to describe their experiences in small groups. Like you, we often cringe when we hear about the inherent power and goodness of small groups (also known by a litany of other names, including community, life, cell, discipleship, home, or grow groups) and compare the idealism of those statements to the reality we've experienced and, embarrassingly, maybe even caused in our own groups, churches, and ministries.

> We've seen groups meet week after week but never move
> beyond the superficial.
> We've seen groups flounder due to a lack of purpose or
> meaning. Before long, members begin disappearing.
> We've seen groups undone by the pressure to multiply; the
> "breakup talk" ultimately did the group in.

We've seen leaders with the best of intentions blunder their
way through conflict, resolving nothing and ultimately
creating more heartache.

We've seen leaders determine to be everything to everyone
within their group and ultimately crash and burn because
they can't live up to those expectations.

We've seen group members fade into oblivion because they
never opened up, or they haven't been engaged, or their
leadership potential goes untapped.

Do any of these describe your experience with groups?

Unfortunately, this is reality for *too many* groups in *too many*
churches. Too many groups struggle, suffer, and then disband.
Maybe you, too, have been disappointed by the reality of groups.
You've encountered unmet expectations or had a bad experience.

Over the years, with so many frustrating group experiences pil-
ing up, most people have learned to simply accept—perhaps without
realizing it—that groups don't deliver as promised. Some have grown
so disillusioned with groups that they will no longer join, let alone
lead one. Others will still join a group, but they'll keep their expectations in check. They don't want to be disappointed once again.
Too many people believe the time and energy of wholly investing in
groups is not worth the hassle.

This seemingly perpetual struggle with groups has led some
churches to give up and try new things. Some pastors have suggested that groups only be used to facilitate introductory friendships
and nothing more.[2] Others have moved away from small groups and
toward deeper Bible teaching through Sunday School, discipleship
institutes, or classes.[3]

SMALL GROUPS ARE (STILL) WORTH IT

Yes, we've observed and experienced many problems with groups,
but we've also seen groups that thrive. We've seen groups where
people take incredible steps forward in their journeys with Jesus,

cultivate deep friendships, and engage in meaningful discipleship relationships.

> We've seen group meetings that are life-changing, group members who develop strong friendships and grow spiritually, and group experiences that exemplify the core discipleship mission of the church.
> We've seen multitudes of people find a sense of belonging because they were invited into a small group.
> We've seen individual group members choose to follow Jesus as their Lord and Savior because of their group experience.
> We've seen unsuspecting people called to leadership and absolutely thrive, discovering a calling they didn't know they had.
> We've seen groups tangibly meet the needs of neighbors, schools, and communities.
> We've seen marriages saved, addictions healed, sin conquered, and lives transformed in and through small groups.
> We've seen small groups become a light that shines into the darkness of this world.

Amazing things are happening every week in small groups in all kinds of churches, ministries, and communities. Because that's what groups are meant to do.

THE POWER OF SMALL GROUPS, THEN AND NOW

Nearly two thousand years ago, the New Testament church took the form of small groups—people gathering together, often in people's homes. Acts 2:42–47 is often seen as the consummate example of how biblical community produces real kingdom growth. Back then, the early church exemplified principles that still apply to today's church. The early church then, and small groups now, when done well, provide the following:

- **Purpose.** The early church committed themselves to teaching, fellowship, the breaking of bread, and prayer (v. 42).
- **Devotion.** The early church was committed daily to its purpose (vv. 42, 46).
- **Shared Ownership.** Everyone in the early church lived with commonality and shared in responsibility for the community (v. 44). The pronouns alone in this passage indicate everyone was "all in."
- **Irresistibility.** The early church's method of daily living contributed to people being added to their groups. They were different, and their uniqueness made them interesting and appealing. They lived in a way that drew others in (v. 47).
- **A place to engage the messiness of life.** The early church made sacrifices, hung in there with each other, and met each other's needs, whatever they were (v. 45).

Today, small groups built on purpose and cultivated by devotion and shared ownership provide an irresistible community wherein people can engage the challenges and the messes of life together. In today's disconnected, fractured society, which has replaced slower communal meals with takeout via Uber Eats (consumed while binging on Netflix), small groups carry on the countercultural tradition that the early church began 2000 years ago, and deliver something far better than the pad thai from the hole-in-the-wall down the street.

Whether they admit it or not, people crave connection. Just look at the abundance of communities built around a healthy lifestyle. People regularly turn to online or face-to-face support groups that normalize difficult experiences and provide communal strategies and support for life's challenges.[4] Rarely will you find anyone living a fitness-driven or recovery-driven life alone. Why? There is power, accountability, and motivation when you are accomplishing something with other people. People are drawn to community, but they often don't know where to find it.

Enter the small group. In light of shifting cultural paradigms and religious orientations, maybe the most countercultural thing the church can do is gather together in small groups. In this "post-Christian era," believers no longer enjoy a culture friendly to or shaped by the church. Exile, which at its very essence is "living away from home,"[5] provides a lens through which the people of God can understand themselves and express the uniqueness of the Christian faith in our current cultural context.

Exile and exilic perspectives aren't new. The people of God—from Daniel in Babylon to the "elect exiles of the Dispersion" (1 Peter 1:1) Peter addressed in his first letter—have always been called to stand apart from the mainstream culture while simultaneously engaging it, offering an alternative way of life. While not all of contemporary culture stands against the church, the first-century church had the reputation of being a place of belonging, strangely accepting of and willing to share in others' burdens, which set Christians apart in the culture in which they lived.

With hospitality and intimacy, we Christians are called to live as exiles in a world that does not affirm us or our faith. A small group that regularly meets together, pursues the Word of God, breaks bread together, and prays together is one powerful response to the culture's shift away from community. It may soon become the most countercultural thing the church does, most attractive to people who don't yet trust Christ but who see and taste true biblical community.[6] That's the promise of small groups.

Small groups do far more than just fulfill a function; they provide a place where people can exemplify God's vision for the church and ultimately live the Christ-following life believers are called to live. For all these reasons, Christians everywhere need to continue to gather and spur one another on toward love and good deeds, as we are encouraged to do in Hebrews 10:23–25:

> . . . let us consider how to stir up one another to love and good works, not neglecting to meet together, as is the habit of some, but encouraging one another, and all the more as you see the Day drawing near.

> We believe that everyday people like you can gather, structure, and build thriving small groups. With intentional and thoughtful leadership, small groups can be—and *should* be—healthy communities that contribute to their members' spiritual growth.

We'll put our cards faceup on the table: we believe in the great potential of small groups. We believe God does some of his best work in small groups as people engage with truth and go on mission together in the midst of community.

We believe that everyday people like you can gather, structure, and build thriving small groups. With intentional and thoughtful leadership, small groups can be—and *should* be—healthy communities that contribute to their members' spiritual growth.

OUR VISION FOR SMALL GROUPS: HEALTHY COMMUNITIES THAT CONTRIBUTE TO INDIVIDUALS' SPIRITUAL GROWTH

Though small groups take all shapes and sizes and forms, our vision for them is the same: healthy communities that contribute to spiritual growth.

Yes, some groups meet weekly in homes to discuss a weekend sermon. Some groups began as a Sunday school class that kept meeting after the class ended. Other groups gather regularly to play basketball or checkers, to go on a hike or a shopping trip, or to make sweaters or socks for kids in a foreign country. Some groups meet at 6 a.m. at a local coffee shop to study the Scriptures. Others meet on Wednesdays at 11 a.m. to watch Jen Wilkin's or Beth Moore's most recent video study. Still others gather after work for fellowship and Bible study well past 9 p.m. Some groups are full of college students who meet in groups facilitated by their campus ministries, others are full of empty nesters, and others take over the neighborhood park when all the families get together.

GROUPS ARE FOR GROWTH

All these groups have something in common: they're interested in helping people grow spiritually in community. No matter how you slice it, people grow into who they're meant to be in the context of community. The Christian life was never meant to be lived alone. The many "one anothers" in the New Testament signal that Christians are meant to live in community: love one another (John 13:34), be at peace with one another (Mark 9:50), bear with and forgive one another (Col. 3:13), regard one another more highly than themselves (Phil. 2:3), speak truth to one another (Eph. 4:25), encourage and build up one another (1 Thess. 5:11), pray for one another (James 5:16), serve one another (Gal. 5:13), and bear one another's burdens (Gal. 6:2).

But community isn't just for community's sake. Ephesians 4:11–16 suggests that the goal of the church is "to equip the saints for the work of the ministry, for building up the body of Christ . . . to grow up in every way into him who is the head." To grow up means to become mature. The goal of community, therefore, is to help "one another" to "grow up" and become spiritually mature. In fact, 90 percent of the pastors we surveyed reported that small groups are the primary means by which discipleship occurs within their church. These pastors have taken to heart what Mark Howell, small groups pastor guru, has said: "Small groups matter because they are the optimal environment for life-change."[7]

Small group members agree. When asked how their small group added value to their life, 65 percent of the small group members we talked to mentioned some element of community, including:

- fellowship and friendship
- care, support, encouragement from the group
- connectedness to the local church and broader church
- similarities shared among group members
- sharing of stories and of the faith

Other participants shared that their small group facilitated deeper biblical knowledge, different perspectives, meaningful discussions, spiritual disciplines, life changes, and accountability, as the table below demonstrates.

CATEGORIES OF SMALL GROUP IMPACT

CATEGORIES OF RESPONSES	WHAT SMALL GROUP MEMBERS SAID
Community	"These people are becoming my friends on a deep level, which I crave. We care for each other, pray for one another, and hold each other accountable. These are real friendships, and we can talk about it all—the minor surface stuff and the deep, sometimes ugly stuff, too." "I feel a part of something. I get something out of it. I have met great people who share and want the same things that I do."
Strengthened Faith	"[My small group] encourages me to grow in my faith and share my faith." "Studying with them helps me with learning and applying God's truth to my life."
Deeper Biblical Knowledge	"[My small group] increases my knowledge of the Word, faith, and my belief system." "I am learning new and different things about God."
Different Perspectives	"[My small group] adds different views on Bible verses, which helps me understand more." "I am learning to appreciate other approaches to responding to God's calling."
Meaningful Discussions	"[My small group] allows me to discuss and verbally talk out my beliefs."
Spiritual Discipline	"It is a meaningful and purposeful mid-week moment to focus on Christ in a crazy, hectic world." "It tangibly brings Jesus and God into my life and marriage, unlike going to church or doing service at church."
Life Change	"It initiated the transformation of my life and has had a major impact on my family's life."
Accountability	"They keep me accountable and encourage me." "They set examples and give good 'reality checks.'"

Certainly, churches and ministries want to help people grow spiritually healthy and mature, and groups provide a context where that can happen because community enables growth.

But those communities also need to be healthy. Abusive homes can produce strong children, but not without significant harm and long-term baggage. Such is the case for groups as well.

GROWTH REQUIRES HEALTHY COMMUNITIES

We want to see spiritual growth occur in healthy communities. We're not looking for perfect communities, but healthy ones. These communities are not surface-level but deep, not clean-cut but messy. Small groups are the places where people following Jesus can engage in the messiness of life together. So, what does a healthy group look like?

Members of healthy groups:

- Know why the group exists and what is most important to the group.
- Consistently attend and demonstrate dedication to the group.
- Share ownership and responsibility for the sustainability of the group.
- Invite authentic conversation, provoking insightful reflections on life and faith.
- Feel free and are invited to share in the ups and downs of life.
- Take care of one another.
- Give and receive grace-driven truth and love.
- Engage difficult conversations for the sake of the gospel and the spurring on of love and good deeds.

Thriving small groups are healthy communities that contribute to individuals' spiritual growth.

That's our vision for small groups. What's yours?

Thriving small groups are healthy communities that contribute to individuals' spiritual growth.

YOUR SMALL GROUP MATTERS

A few years ago, in the midst of a churchwide study, Kenton and Laura[8] felt a nudge to start a small group and invite three other couples with whom they wanted to connect more. Within a few weeks, those couples invited other couples. Eventually that group of eight grew to twelve, all because one couple felt compelled to start a group and followed through with it.

As the group continued to meet and grow, members began to serve within the church and found ways to serve with a local organization. A year later, Kenton and Laura decided that baptism was the next step in their walk with Jesus. Four other couples in their group decided the same thing. All at once, one right after another, this small group experienced ten baptisms! One act of obedience, inviting a few people to start a small group, led to additional, beautiful acts of obedience.

Your small group has the same potential.

Millions of people in all types of churches want to participate with other people, to learn and grow in their walk with Jesus. We owe it to them, and we owe it to the Lord, to humbly but boldly figure out how to lead small groups well.

We owe it to them, and we owe it to the Lord, to humbly but boldly figure out how to lead small groups well.

Yes, leading and cultivating thriving small groups is challenging, but small groups have the potential to change individuals and their communities, and to provide the means by which they can effectively live out a Christian life. In groups, God gives us, as small group leaders, opportunities to participate with him in transforming lives with the help of the Holy Spirit when we are willing to obey and lead courageously. Yes, this journey will require you to make a great investment, but it will also come with a great reward.

Let's get to work!

GROUPS DO WHAT PASTORS CAN'T

Tim Lucas

As a lead pastor, I've heard all of the platitudes about why small groups are essential to the life of a growing church. *Life is better in community. Groups are how to make a big church feel small.* Heck, I've said many of them myself! Since launching Liquid Church in 2007, we've experienced our share of both struggles and successes with groups. But the robust spiritual care small groups provide for our people is worth our staff's effort to gain sustainable traction.

Far beyond a fill-in-the-blanks Bible study or weekly prayer circle, small groups provide extraordinary soul care for people who experience unexpected crises, as my friend Rosa did. Rosa and her husband, Fabian, were expecting their first child. Rosa had two children from a previous marriage, and they were thrilled to be adding a new baby of their own. One day, as Rosa was taking her daughter to a ballet recital, something didn't feel right. She wasn't feeling the baby move and was having unusual cramping. At the doctor's office the next day, she discovered the horrific truth: the baby had died in utero. Devastated, Rosa and Fabian delivered a stillborn child.

To make matters worse, Rosa contracted a muscular disorder that caused her to be bedridden and unable to care for her family following the stillbirth. Depressed, discouraged, and carrying feelings of guilt and failure, she and Fabian wondered where God was and how they could possibly go on.

As pastors, we know that this type of crisis can shake the faith of even the strongest believer. In devastating situations like this, there are few words even the most experienced pastor can share to provide adequate comfort. Hospital visits, prayers with the family, and even checking in via text or email simply won't be enough. That's where Rosa and Fabian's small group stepped up to minister to this vulnerable family.

Rosa's small group sprang into action. They quickly arranged a schedule to drive Rosa's kids back and forth from school, transport them to sports and dance events, and bring them to social activities at their own homes or at our church to give Rosa and Fabian a break. "Fabulous meals began appearing night after night," Rosa recalled. They did the family's laundry and cleaned their house. "It felt like I had an army of angels by my side," Rosa said. As the small group rallied around Rosa's family, they became the tangible hands and feet of Jesus, reminding her of God's sustaining love during a season of darkness and loss.

Truth be told, there is not one pastor on our staff—including myself—who could have done all that for Rosa and Fabian as effectively and consistently as their small group did. The hands-on spiritual care the small group provided Monday through Friday ministered more powerfully than any sermon or service we could architect on a Sunday.

Andy Stanley says that circles are stronger than rows, and I agree. This is why we make small groups such a priority at Liquid Church. We understand that the depth of care and discipleship that happens in groups simply can't happen anywhere else in the life of the church.

Because we believe so much in the power of small groups, we stage a "Groups Sunday" twice a year at all seven of our church campuses. As lead pastor, I preach a shortened message about the power of community and give a preview of what our small groups will be studying for the next seven weeks. We end the service early (a miracle!) and release our multisite congregation of 5,000 to go out into their lobbies for a small groups expo where they can meet group leaders face-to-face and sign up for a group. As a recent newbie named Rod explained:

If you hadn't cut the service short and made me walk out of the auditorium to meet the small group leaders, I never would have joined a group. Being a part of my group has been life-changing. Not only do we have fun studying the Bible (which I never thought I would say), but when my teenager went off the deep end, our group came alongside us with wisdom and prayer. They even talked to our teen in a way he would hear! He trusted them because they came to our house week after week and became family. Our entire family began to live for Christ in a way we never have before! I don't know what I would do without these precious people.

Be encouraged: we struggled for years to get healthy small groups off the ground. Testimonies were hard to come by at first. But now, testimonies of life-change and soul care are part of almost every small group story at Liquid Church!

———————

Tim Lucas is the founder and lead pastor of Liquid Church, one of America's fastest-growing churches, and author of *Liquid Church: Six Powerful Currents to Saturate Your City for Christ.* Learn more at LiquidChurch.com.

KEY TAKEAWAYS

1. Small groups built on purpose and cultivated by devotion and shared ownership provide:
   - A place to engage the challenges and messes of life together
   - A context in which people can grow spiritually together
   - An example of an attractive, irresistible community to an unbelieving world
   - A way for the Church to live counterculturally

2. Thriving small groups of all shapes, sizes, and forms are healthy communities that contribute to individuals' spiritual growth.

3. Community is always built around something. Small group communities are best built to encourage spiritual growth.

REFLECTION AND DISCUSSION QUESTIONS

1. ✋ **Remember:** What caught your attention in this chapter about thriving small groups?

2. 🦉 **Understand:** Why are groups so important?

3. ✳️ **Apply:** What are the various "visions" for small groups you have heard in churches and ministries over the years? How do those compare to the vision outlined in this chapter?

4. 🔍 **Analyze:** Considering their challenges, are small groups worth it? Why or why not?

5. 💡 **Create:** Think about the group you are leading or getting ready to lead. What is your vision for your group? Use the following questions to help get you started:

   a. 🦉 **Understand:** What does a spiritually healthy follower of Jesus Christ look like to you?

   b. ✳️ **Apply:** How can your group help its members grow into that kind of Christ-follower?

   c. ✳️ **Apply:** What does a "healthy" group look like for you?

   d. 🔍 **Analyze:** If the group were to end, years down the road, what do you hope will have happened in the lives of your group members because you met together regularly?

CHAPTER 2

WHAT DOES A CATALYTIC LEADER DO?

Painting a Picture of Next-Level Group Leadership

Your measure as a leader is not what you do,
but what others do because of what you do.

—HOWIE HENDRICKS

Many potential leaders make the mistake of thinking that their success as a leader rests upon how well they perform certain tasks, like teaching a killer Bible study or answering vexing questions posed by group members. They believe bestselling leadership expert and former pastor John Maxwell's famous maxim: "Everything rises and falls on leadership." But they are using the wrong measuring stick.

They are measuring leadership success by how they perform and what they do. Scholars often refer to the romance of leadership when discussing the role and impact of leaders on their organizations' success. Years ago, management scholar Jim Meindl explained that many of us "hold the view that leadership is a central organizational process and the premier force in the scheme of organizational events and activities,"[1] and thereby de-emphasize the contributions of other individuals, environments, or markets, and other contributors to organizational or group success.

This belief is a problem because sometimes leaders don't matter as much as people think. Rebellious kids can come from the homes of great parents. Linebackers can commit bone-headed penalties and cause their well-led team to lose on the final drive of a game. People cheat on their spouses and their taxes, even in gospel-centered churches that clearly teach the entire Word of God. Certainly, leaders matter a lot, but so do the actions of those who follow them. These people make their own choices irrespective of their leaders. In fact, follow-up studies over the years have suggested that formal team leaders only account for 15 percent or so of a group's performance.[2] However, the merging of all team or organizational members' contributions and how the entire group works cooperatively makes a much greater difference.

However, the merging of all team or organizational members' contributions and how the entire group works cooperatively makes a much greater difference.

So not everything is in your control, but as a leader you *are* responsible for inviting and encouraging group members' contributions and group-level cooperation. As Howie Hendricks aptly stated in the quote introducing this chapter, your leadership isn't just about what you do, but what others do *because* of what you do. In other words, your leadership success can be judged by looking at the people you lead. What are *they* doing? Are *their* lives making an impact? Are *they* growing and being transformed? And more importantly, are their lives impacting the lives of others?

You can lead in a way that invites people—both within your group and outside of your group—to help your group become a place where people can grow into who God has designed them to be. When that happens, it'll be for their good, their community's good, and God's glory. We want to teach you how to be the kind of catalytic group leader who profoundly impacts the people God has entrusted to your care.

If you want to be a next-level leader, you will:

- Clarify your group's mission and relentlessly pursue it while holding at bay attempts to detract from it.
- Set the stage for community, discipleship, and mission, and then make sure you get out of the way of what God wants to do.
- Promote others in your group and encourage them to make the maximal contribution they can.
- Facilitate life-changing dialogue and discussions rather than dominating the group conversation.
- Set up and cultivate a group structure that best promotes your group's engagement.
- Ask good questions and point group discussions back to accomplishing your group's unique purpose.
- Not only take care of yourself but continue to sharpen your leadership and facilitation skill set to help your group grow.
- Release your iron grip on the reins of leadership, invite others to join you in leading, and then turn things over to them when they're ready.

Now, this list may feel like a lot. It may seem like a high calling. Well, it is! You are critically important to your group, especially if you want members to move beyond superficial relationships and reviewing answers to the week's Bible study. In fact, in our study, we found that a leader's commitment to the group is one of the strongest predictors of a small group's effectiveness.[3]

A leader's commitment to the group is one of the strongest predictors of a small group's effectiveness.

This means two things. *First*, you can make a tremendous impact on your group simply by showing up. *Second*, if you want to be a leader whose leadership transforms others, you must be committed.

When we asked leaders of the most effective groups in our study how they demonstrated their commitment to their groups, most of what we heard was what you'd expect:

I show up.

I know what's going on in their lives. And I follow up with them with a quick text or call.

I keep a prayer list on my phone, and I schedule times to pray for my group.

I reach out if someone misses a meeting.

I do the same things I ask them to do (like reading assignments during the week).

I take the group meetings seriously. I prepare for them and consistently attend them.

I admit when I don't know things. I am willing to be honest about my shortcomings.

I get involved in what they are doing and show that they are important to me.

I take the lead in being open and honest. It helps everyone else do the same.

Keep in mind that not every leader does all of these things. But this list gives you a picture of what commitment looks like: showing up, preparing, caring, reaching out. These are simple things that take time and effort, but they make all the difference.

When you're deeply committed to your group, you'll be the kind of leader who has the potential to make a massive difference. You don't need titles or crowns of blessing or mantles of leadership. You need to demonstrate commitment.

Two key factors that help leaders develop greater commitment and therefore cultivate more effective groups are coaching and training.[4] Leaders who receive effective coaching and training are far more equipped to lead their groups than those who do not.

There's no way around it—the quality of leaders makes a huge impact on individual groups and the systems of which they're a part.

Successful, transformational small groups are catalyzed by committed leaders.

In this chapter, we'll introduce you to the *Leading Small Groups That Thrive* model, explain what pastors and group members are looking for from you as a leader, outline the roles you will play as a group leader, and discuss what leaders do that matters most, all with the goal of helping you become a catalytic, next-level group leader.

CATALYTIC LEADERSHIP

Great group leaders play a catalytic function. Ideally, you demonstrate a deep commitment to your group, communicate regularly with your group members, and show care for your group members. From there, leaders take particular actions that result in thriving small group experiences. By prioritizing five key actions, you can catalyze your leadership and help your group grow into a healthy community that contributes to individuals' spiritual growth.

THE LEADING SMALL GROUPS THAT THRIVE MODEL

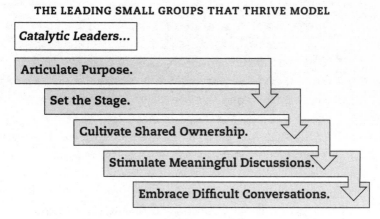

1. **Articulate Purpose.** To be a catalytic leader, you must know your group's unique purpose, prioritize what matters most, and continually refocus the group to pursue its purpose. To help your group thrive, clearly articulate a compelling purpose and then pursue it with fervor and commitment.

2. **Set the Stage.** To be a catalytic leader, set the stage for incredible group experiences as you gather people together and start your group. Pay attention to group size, gather people with intentionality, structure your group to support its purpose, and establish communication norms that set the stage for effective engagement. To help your group thrive, provide the motivation and the structure for deeper engagement, and create a space where devoted people can pursue their unique purpose together.

3. **Cultivate Shared Ownership.** To be a catalytic leader, you must invite and inspire group members to continually deepen their commitment, spur members to share life with one another, and communicate frequently. To help your group thrive, cultivate an environment wherein committed members know and care for one another and take on increasing leadership roles within the group.

4. **Stimulate Meaningful Discussions.** To be a catalytic leader, you must facilitate fantastic conversations. Ask great questions, contribute but let your group members shine, and facilitate meaningful group discussions. To help your group thrive, strive to generate robust, challenging, and fruitful conversations driven by the entire group's full engagement.

5. **Embrace Difficult Conversations.** To be a catalytic leader, don't avoid or stifle conflict and tension. Instead, cultivate mutual accountability and leverage healthy tension for the good of group members and the group as a whole. To help your group thrive, create a culture where your group is free to not only experience conflict, but lean into it and grow from it together.

Now, we don't want to oversimplify these matters. Every one of these elements is complex, and you need wisdom to apply them appropriately in different circumstances. We'll unpack each of these practices further in future chapters. But for now, we've kept this model simple so that you know what you need to focus on in your journey toward being an outstanding small group leader. Certainly, every choice you make for your group has ramifications. We trust that you—as you listen to the Holy Spirit and to wise counsel—will know how to determine what's best for your particular group. Our hope is that this research-driven *Leading Small Groups That Thrive* model will help you, as a leader, focus your time and energy on actions that lead to transformational small group experiences that contribute to individuals' spiritual growth.

To put the five elements of the *Leading Small Groups That Thrive* model into action, you will play, by yourself or in partnership with others in your group, several key roles as you lead your group.

KEY ROLES GROUP LEADERS FULFILL

Integrity, teachability, and spiritual maturity. We've crunched the data, and these three traits are what pastors prioritize when they look for potential group leaders. While this might not surprise you, it might be worth considering what they are *not* prioritizing: teaching, mentoring, leading, and gathering skills. In the bar chart below, each bar represents the percentage of pastors in our study who rated the specific qualification as important or very important when looking for potential small group leaders.

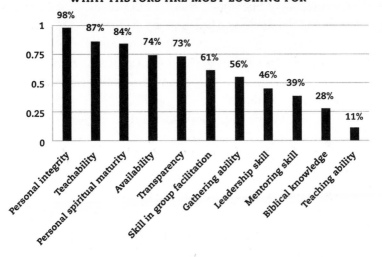

WHAT PASTORS ARE MOST LOOKING FOR

Pastors look for spiritually mature, teachable people with integrity who may or may not come with the actual skills needed to effectively gather and lead a group. At the same time, our data revealed that the members of groups in which individuals grew the most viewed their leaders as smart, concerned, and caring.

To be the kind of leader your group will need to thrive, you'll either have to play many roles or develop a team of leaders who are able to meet many competing demands. The way you engage these roles will depend on the kind of group you lead as well as your church's or ministry's expectations for small group leadership.

As you contemplate your call to group leadership, consider these seven small group leader roles:

Visionary—Many people come into a group because their pastor said they should on Sunday morning, or because a friend invited them. But they have no real vision for what role the group could play in their life. You get to help them envision what could be: the kinds of friendships they could cultivate; the way God could speak truth, life, and grace to them in the context of the group; the kind of impact they could have on others inside and outside the group. Visionaries don't just see what is; they see what could be.

Gatherer—At least initially, small group leaders play a gathering role. You invite and welcome people into your group, your life, and often, your home. We recognize that pulling your group together and launching it successfully may be particularly challenging for more introverted leaders.

Discussion Facilitator—Great discussions generally don't happen naturally. They are thoughtfully planned and carefully cultivated and nourished. Great facilitators know how to ask great questions, how to design the space for maximum impact, and how to manage group members who dominate, distract, or withdraw. To facilitate literally means to "make easy," and you are responsible for making group discussions easy and meaningful.

Logistics Organizer—Someone has to manage the details. When are we meeting? Where? What are we eating and drinking? What are we doing with the kids? Oftentimes these duties are managed by the person who opens their home, patio, or backyard to their group. These issues matter a lot to people's ability and willingness to commit to a group. Without well-managed logistics, many people will simply withdraw. Plus, well-planned logistics create an atmosphere that promotes connection and meaningful interaction.

Intercessor (Pray-er)—Especially when your group is first coming together, you will be the one to cover your group in prayer. Even after other group members join in, leaders of groups that contribute to members' spiritual growth the most pray regularly for their group members, both during and outside of group gatherings.

Spiritual Guide/Teacher—Many groups study the Bible or a Christian living book, which often puts the leader in a teaching role. Apart from formal teaching roles, many group members look to the leader as a person who both models what healthy spirituality looks like and can help them on their journey of spiritual growth. Group members often look to their leader to spiritually guide or teach them in some way.

Peacemaker—Good groups struggle. They fight. They experience awkward moments. That's part of the deal. Just as you wouldn't want a best friend with whom you never disagree, you don't want a group that *never* gets a little sideways. Often, groups look to their leader to take on a peacemaking role when tensions arise. Your effectiveness in doing so might be the determining factor in how the group responds and moves forward once the dust settles.

We realize that not everyone who volunteers to be a leader will be skilled and/or comfortable with each of these roles. That's okay. Catalytic leaders create space for others to step into and contribute in these areas and others—and even to take on more and different leadership roles as time goes on. Remember, it's less about what you do and more about what others do because of your next-level group leadership.

In combination with at least one of the roles above, you will play a shepherding role, caring for the sheep in your flock. As Chris Surratt explained in Leading Small Groups,[5] shepherds lead from the heart, with compassion, out in front of the group, and sacrificially. If you are up for that, then you have the makings of a fantastic leader.

The following assessment will help you identify your areas of strength. It will also help you identify which areas will require extra attention and energy. Once you've identified your weaknesses, consider gathering a team of leaders who can fill in the gaps, allowing you to more fully operate in your strengths while ensuring your group has what it needs to move to the next level.

LEADERS NEED HELP

While there are many roles to play, it's less important that you eloquently unpack passages of Scripture and more important that you facilitate a conversation in which others are able to dig into that passage. It's less important that you have good answers to your group members' questions and more important that you are able to draw out great answers from others in the group. In other words, great leaders realize they haven't taught anything unless others have learned, and they haven't led unless others have followed. Your leadership should be defined by catalyzing the actions of others. Acting with this truth in mind is what can make you an amazing leader.

A well-equipped leader is able to lead in such a way that his or her group contributes substantially to every group member's spiritual growth. When leaders aren't properly equipped, their groups fail to gain traction and build momentum. Groups start strong but quickly fizzle out. Leaders grow overwhelmed and drop out. And when ministries don't have enough well-equipped leaders, small

LEADERSHIP ROLE STRENGTHS ASSESSMENT

HOW WELL DOES EACH STATEMENT BELOW DESCRIBE YOU?			
VISIONARY ✳	NOT AT ALL ME	SORTA ME	YES, THAT'S MY JAM!
I tend to be consumed with thoughts and ideas of what could be, both for myself and others.			1
I know the impact of groups, and I envision the potential impact for small groups on people's lives.			1
I can clearly articulate the purpose of my small group.			1
Count the number of marks in each column, and multiply them by the number in this row. Then add up the columns.	× 1	× 2	× 3
Total: 9 (sum)	0 +	0 +	9
GATHERER	NOT AT ALL ME	SORTA ME	YES, THAT'S MY JAM!
I often have lots of people over for socializing at my house.	1		
I enjoy introducing people who don't yet know each other to one another and watching them become friends.		1	
People often wonder how I have so much time to engage with so many people.	1		
Count the number of marks in each column, and multiply them by the number in this row. Then add up the columns.	× 1	× 2	× 3
Total: 4 (sum)	2 +	2 +	0
DISCUSSION FACILITATOR ✳	NOT AT ALL ME	SORTA ME	YES, THAT'S MY JAM!
If no one else is going to lead the group, I will.			1
I love asking good, hard, meaningful questions of my friends.			1
My friends tell me I ask great questions.			1
Count the number of marks in each column, and multiply them by the number in this row. Then add up the columns.	× 1	× 2	× 3
Total: 9 (sum)	0 +	0 +	9
LOGISTICS ORGANIZER	NOT AT ALL ME	SORTA ME	YES, THAT'S MY JAM!
I love preparing my home so it is welcoming and inviting to guests.			1
My friends tell me I should be a professional organizer.	1		
I have systems and processes that work to handle all the stuff that needs to be organized for my life and/or our group (e.g., meals, kids).		1	
Count the number of marks in each column, and multiply them by the number in this row. Then add up the columns.	× 1	× 2	× 3
Total: 6 (sum)	1 +	2 +	3

INTERCESSOR (PRAY-ER)	NOT AT ALL ME	SORTA ME	YES, THAT'S MY JAM!
I regularly and systematically pray for important people in my life.			\
People ask me to pray for them because they know my reputation as a prayer warrior.		)	
I feel confident in helping others learn how to pray.	)		
Count the number of marks in each column, and multiply them by the number in this row. Then add up the columns.	× 1	× 2	× 3
Total: ___6___ (sum)	1 +	2 +	3
SPIRITUAL GUIDE/TEACHER	NOT AT ALL ME	SORTA ME	YES, THAT'S MY JAM!
I know my Bible and feel equipped to apply it to my life and others' lives.			\
I've taught or facilitated Bible or book studies before, so I know what I'm doing.		\	
People come to me for spiritual advice and mentorship.			\
Count the number of marks in each column, and multiply them by the number in this row. Then add up the columns.	× 1	× 2	× 3
Total: ___8___ (sum)	0 +	2 +	6
PEACEMAKER	NOT AT ALL ME	SORTA ME	YES, THAT'S MY JAM!
I revel in seeing people who are in conflict come to resolution and restored relationship.			\
I lean into and not away from tension in relationships.			\
People say I'm willing to say what needs to be said, no matter how awkward it makes the situation.		\	
Count the number of marks in each column, and multiply them by the number in this row. Then add up the columns.	× 1	× 2	× 3
Total: ___8___ (sum)	0 +	2 +	6
Star your top 2 scored roles.			
Circle your bottom 2 scored roles.			
What insights does this tool offer you?			

groups cannot proliferate. In too many churches, there are people who want to join groups but too few leaders to create space for them to join.

However, when a church or ministry deploys a sufficient number of well-equipped leaders, a small groups ministry can flourish. People begin to realize who they really are as they grasp their identity in Christ. People experience authentic community where they can truly grow and address issues and challenges in their lives. People are equipped and encouraged to live differently in every facet of life. When this happens, groups live up to their promise, cultivating a dynamic environment where group members begin to understand and actualize who God is calling them to be.

We want to help raise up an army of well-equipped leaders who can lead thriving, transformational, next-level small groups. When we asked, small group leaders told us what they need help with most:

1. Encouraging commitment among group members
2. Cultivating good discussion and engagement
3. Coordinating logistics
4. Maintaining a strong personal walk with God
5. Sharing leadership and developing other leaders

Do you need help in these areas, too?

In addition, small groups pastors and ministry leaders also recognize the need to effectively resource leaders. To put it simply, *you consume your pastors' thoughts.* When we asked small groups pastors their biggest needs related to small groups ministry, the top five needs were:

1. Assessing groups and the small groups ministry
2. Developing leaders
3. Coaching and caring for leaders
4. Recruiting leaders
5. Multiplying groups

Except for assessment, it's pretty much all about leaders. They're looking after you, and they're directing their efforts toward you all the time.

In the following chapters, we offer practical strategies for how to plan for, launch, build, and sustain highly effective, transformational small group experiences that will help your members grow spiritually.

TAKE YOUR NEXT STEP

Your call to lead a group of people toward community, discipleship, and mission is a big deal. Groups are places where God does some of his best work, and leaders are essential in creating environments where people can grow into the catalytic people they're designed to be.

You matter a lot to both your group members and your church and ministry leaders.

Most likely, the people you lead are putting a lot of stock in what you do and don't do. They may be attributing too much power and impact to you (you know, the leadership attribution error), but right or wrong, they *are* looking to you.

You and what you do matters a lot. As mentioned earlier in this chapter, our study found that one of the strongest predictors of a small group's effectiveness was the leader's commitment to the group. While this may be a product of the romance of leadership, ultimately, your group members think your commitment matters. And that's a big deal!

As a leader, you can increase your impact on the group you lead when you encourage and facilitate your group's contributions and engagement.

You might feel ill-equipped to lead your group. Maybe you're nervous—how is this going to go? Maybe you feel like the least spiritual member of your group—how are you going to lead them? Maybe this is your first time leading—how will they trust you and allow you to lead?

Start by affirming your commitment. Then, take a few minutes to ask God to give you strength as you engage as a leader, and perhaps talk though your *Leadership Roles Strength Assessment* and your answers to the Reflection and Discussion Questions below with a friend or two. Then, let's move forward in building and strengthening a thriving small group.

GROUP LEADER, YOUR GROUPS PASTOR WANTS YOU TO KNOW

Mark Howell

Years ago, many of us in pastoral ministry realized that small groups provide "the optimal environment for the life-change Jesus intends for every believer."[6]

I've been facilitating small groups and leading small groups ministries for twenty-five years, and consulting with small groups pastors for the past ten years, and I can tell you that life-change happens best when groups are led by great leaders. You matter so much to the health of your group, the growth of your group members, and the growth and flourishing of your small groups ministry.

And I know enough small groups pastors to know that yours agrees.

Here are eight things I think your small groups pastor wants you to know about the impact you make on those you lead and the churches and ministries of which you are a part:

1. **You model what it looks like to follow Jesus.** Life-change only happens when Jesus does a work in us. You show group members that while following Jesus includes learning about him, knowledge is not the end in mind. Following is the end in mind. Therefore, while learning is involved, becoming is primary. Not simply *trying* to become like Jesus, but *training* to become like him.

2. **You create inclusive environments.** Jesus' first invitation was "Come and see." You invite people to do the same. In fact, the value of "Come as you are" is deeply woven into the fabric of inclusivity.

3. **You encourage intentional conversations and gatherings.** Not only is your group inclusive, but you bring forth an expectation of movement. "Come as you are . . . and don't stay that way" is at the heart of life-change. You ask your group members, "What is your next step?" and help them intentionally pursue growth.

4. **You create safe environments wherein transparency is the rule, not the exception.** Your group isn't a place where "all's well" or a pseudo-community where people gather with masks on. Instead, you encourage the real person to show up, mess and all, and pursue life-change.

5. **You cultivate environments where people can dialogue and explore the truth of God's Word and how it applies to their lives.** Monologues are often efficient for distributing information, but they are rarely effective at producing the personal clarity and conviction that lead to next steps. You create spaces for dialogue and discussion that prompt learning and application.

6. **You facilitate a sense of connection far beyond weekend services and even beyond your group meetings.** Certainly what happens during weekend services or during group meetings is important. But what happens between meetings is the secret ingredient that enables the life-on-life engagement Jesus' closest followers experienced (as did Paul's). When you share life with your group members (i.e., a meal, a cup of coffee, a text message or a Facebook message to encourage, a phone call just to connect), you facilitate connections that result in life-change.

7. **You create a community where people can practice the "one-anothers" (e.g., Rom. 12:10, 2 Cor. 13:11, Eph. 4:32).** This was the primary activity of the early church, but it gets obscured in our hyper-busy culture. But you create a space and a community where this happens. The love Jesus spoke

of in John 13:34–35 was far beyond verbal. Far more important than a hug and an "I love you, brother" is countercultural one-anothering.

8. **You extend your church's or ministry's shepherding capacity.** Your pastors cannot effectively reach and care for everyone in your church. But when you step forward and shepherd your small group, your tribe, you dramatically grow the church's capacity to love and care for people.

For all these reasons and more, the reality is that your church (or ministry) couldn't be what it is without your commitment, investment, and modeling of what it means to follow Jesus and pursue growth in community with others.

On behalf of your pastor or ministry, thank you for your leadership and your desire to grow in your capacity to lead well, clearly shown by the fact that you are reading these words!

Mark Howell is the pastor of communities at Canyon Ridge Christian Church in Las Vegas, Nevada, and founder of SmallGroupResources.net. Connect at MarkHowellLive.com.

KEY TAKEAWAYS

1. Remember that the real measure of your leadership is not what you do, but what others do because of what you do.
2. Recognize that your commitment to your group can significantly contribute to the spiritual growth of your members.
3. Focus on catalyzing the actions of others in your group.
4. Take your leadership role seriously, but don't make it all about you.
5. Don't try to do it all yourself. Even now, consider into what leadership roles you can invite others to help you.

REFLECTION AND DISCUSSION QUESTIONS

1. 🖐 **Remember:** Why did you agree to lead a small group? If you're not currently leading a group, what is causing you to consider leading a small group?
2. 🖐 **Remember:** What caught your attention in this chapter about great small group leaders?
3. 🦉 **Understand:** What do you now understand comprises great small group leadership?
4. ⚙ **Apply:** After taking the Leadership Roles Strength Assessment, which role(s) do you consider current areas of strength?
5. ⚙ **Apply:** After taking the Leadership Roles Strength Assessment, which role(s) will you need to devote extra attention and energy to or gather others around you with those strengths?
6. 📋 **Evaluate:** Which is a bigger pitfall for you in leading others: (a) self-righteousness and pride or (b) inadequacy and unbelief in God's work through you?

CHAPTER 3

HOW DO I GET WHERE I WANT TO GO?

Mapping a Plan to Develop a Thriving Group

What got you here won't get you there.

—MARSHALL GOLDSMITH

Long before the days of Google Maps was the AAA Triptik. Before summer vacation, Ryan's dad would visit the local Automobile Club office. The staff there would lay out his family's entire trip plan and produce a little booklet that would tell them where they were, how far they'd gone, how far they had to go, and what interesting sights were coming up. Those Triptiks brought two essential elements to their journey: a plan and peace.

Today, while our phones perform many of the same functions as a Triptik, many of us still appreciate a good roadmap. Roadmaps provide a plan for where we're going and peace when we find ourselves on a winding mountain road or a long, empty stretch of desert. They help us know we're on the right track.

Group leaders need a roadmap, too. Without one, they lack a

plan and the peace it provides. Fortunately, there's a great body of research that has thoroughly explored the journey groups take to become productive and meaningful. Group development research outlines the stages of that journey and suggests how group leaders can help their groups grow more effectively.

We've found the research on group development—studies that examine how some groups move through stages to good performance, while others don't—to be incredibly instructive. Perhaps you've heard of the Forming–Storming–Norming–Performing model before. That's group development, too! But the literature here is far more rich and insightful than most of us know. This chapter provides a crash course that will immediately help you start or restart your small group well, and will provide a necessary conceptual foundation for much of what will follow in this book. Even if you've heard of the "-ormings" before, don't skip over this chapter, as we're sure there will be new insights for you along the way!

THE BASIC ARGUMENTS FROM GROUP DEVELOPMENT RESEARCH

Before we get into the stages of group development, let's lay out the foundational ideas that the body of research on group development tells us.

Your group will likely need to move through various stages to get to a place of rich community and spiritual growth. Sometimes, that may feel like a lack of progress. Keep in mind that moving to a place of rich growth tends to take six months or more, even for groups that meet or serve together on a daily basis. It may take a group that meets every week or two even longer to move to a place of productivity—and many of your groups won't even be together for more than a few months simply because of the design of your church small groups ministry.

Even though groups tend to take a long time to become great, there are many things you can do as a leader to facilitate and catalyze your group's development. You will need to provide dramatically different kinds of leadership to your group at various stages as there is no "one-size-fits-all" approach here.

Groups that fail to accomplish the functions necessary to move from one stage to the next either stagnate or disband. Research into group development not only provides us with insights into subpar group experiences, but it helps us develop tools to diagnose what's going wrong, as well as to identify the right prescription for healing and growth.

Typically, groups progress through three stages before they begin to function optimally in a fourth stage of performance and production. Psychologist Susan Wheelan[1] describes the stages as follows:

> **Stage 1: Inclusion and Dependency.** As a group initially comes together, group members are seeking to identify acceptable behavior in the group, and they are looking to the established leader to tell them what to do and make them feel comfortable.
>
> **Stage 2: Counterdependency and Conflict.** Once people feel comfortable, the group begins to debate issues of power and authority, what they want to accomplish, and how they want to actually work and be together in the group. If the conflict that ensues is managed well (and engaged, not squashed), good things happen, including constructive relationships, cohesion among members, and refined group values. All of these propel the group forward.
>
> **Stage 3: Trust and Structure.** Out of conflict experienced in the second stage, trusting relationships develop, and the group engages in more mature and open communication and negotiation regarding group goals, roles, and structures.
>
> **Stage 4: Work and Productivity.** The group is concerned with what they want to get done and who they want to be. The group enjoys an open exchange of ideas about the task and achieves its goals as it works together. We like to refer to this stage as "the promised land."

STAGES OF GROUP DEVELOPMENT

Group Development: What does it look like?

Inclusion + Dependency

Counterdependency + Conflict

Trust + Structure

Work + Productivity

By understanding what needs to happen in each stage before the group can move on to the next stage, members and leaders are able to focus their energies on actions that help the group progress. We'll help you understand what group members are looking for and how you can provide those things as a leader.

STAGE 1: STARTING WELL THROUGH INCLUSIVE AND DIRECTIVE LEADERSHIP

Stage 1 is called *Inclusion and Dependency* for very good reasons. When people first come into a group, they are concerned about their psychological safety and feeling included. Group members in this stage are also dependent on the leader.

To assuage their fears about fitting in or acting appropriately within the group, new members seek order and structure so they can know what behavior is expected of them. They're not yet ready to fully and openly contribute; they need their leader to help them know what is expected and give them opportunities to contribute.

Leaders ignore these realities at their peril. Embracing them provides the leadership their group needs. When your group is first coming together, you need to create a sense of belonging and establish predictable patterns of behavior. This will help people feel secure enough to keep coming and, when they come, to contribute their own thoughts and feelings.

At this stage, many leaders are tempted to become too passive or too dominant.

A passive leader too quickly asks the group members what they want out of the group, simultaneously withholding his or her own participation, with the hope that others can find plenty of space to talk and contribute. But new groups or new group members aren't ready for that yet. They need direction.

By contrast, dominant leaders come with a printed agenda, have a rigid plan for the group's time together, and immediately fill every bit of awkward silence. They may appear too rigid, with too much organized in advance, and as if they have a lot to teach group members. This leadership may produce passive followers who are insecure about what they're able to contribute. They may come to the group for the purpose of being taught, rather than becoming engaged members who are willing and ready to contribute to the group and the other members' spiritual growth.

Great leaders avoid this dilemma by being *directive* as their group comes together. Your thoughtful leadership will show new members that you have a plan for the group, and they'll breathe a sigh of relief. Your intentional leadership will also offer space for people to feel like they belong in the group. We'll offer specifics on what that looks like in chapter 5. For now, remember that at this initial stage of your group development, people are dependent on the designated leaders, so give them the directive leadership they need and want.

If Stage 1 goes well, your group members will develop a feeling of loyalty to the group and want to belong to it and one another, and they'll feel safe enough to offer ideas and suggestions to help the group accomplish its goals.

STAGE 2: CULTIVATING EMERGENT CONFLICT AND DEVELOPING A GROUP CLIMATE

When group members feel comfortable and understand that their group's structure encourages (rather than shuts down) their contributions, they will likely grow comfortable speaking up and sharing their ideas. Oftentimes, however, their ideas conflict with how you as a leader or other group members do things, and thus, conflict emerges. That's why Stage 2 is termed *Counterdependency and Conflict*. No longer only dependent on their leader, group members share their own ideas, which causes conflict in the group.

But this conflict is a good thing. In fact, it's essential!

For instance, a leader might arrange for her group to meet on Tuesdays from 7–8:30 p.m. at a local Starbucks. But during the third or fourth meeting, a member realizes that she doesn't feel super comfortable sharing her struggles with her husband in such a public setting and suggests that Starbucks might not be the best meeting place. Someone else agrees, and another person suggests starting the group at 8 p.m. because that would give her the chance to put her kids to bed before meeting. Yet another member starts to raise some challenging theological questions that don't exactly line up with the stated church doctrine and "What we believe" statements. Soon, everyone is sharing their opinions and wishes.

In these situations, it's common (and understandable) for a leader to feel slightly offended. But instead of shutting down her members' ideas, she should welcome the feedback and allow the group to work together to solve the problem of when and where to meet and how to tackle challenging topics. That will enable the group to move out of Stage 1 and into and through Stage 2.

Here are a few tips to lead effectively as your group grows comfortable enough to contribute and push back on your leadership.

DON'T BE A FIXER; ALLOW THE GROUP TO NEGOTIATE THROUGH THEIR CONFLICTS.

As conflicts surface, resist the urge to resolve them yourself by making executive decisions. Instead, facilitate discussions in which the group works through their differences of opinion and comes to an agreement. (By the way, we devote all of chapter 8 to helping you leverage tension and deal effectively with conflict in your group.) Not only will your group collectively decide how they want the group to work, but you will also establish a norm of group participation and engagement. Your group will begin to collectively establish a group culture—one that is far stronger than you could create on your own.

RESIST THE URGE TO TAKE PUSH-BACK PERSONALLY.
Great leaders throw their arms wide open and welcome challenges to the structure they've established. Even if you feel defensive, don't show it. If you assert your authority to the exclusion of your group members, you will shut down members who want to contribute, tempting them to take their talents elsewhere. Even when a group member proposes an outlandish idea, welcome the criticism and engage your group in conversation by saying something like, "That's an interesting idea. What do you all think about Jennifer's suggestion? How would you like to proceed here?"

If Stage 2 goes well, your group members will gain a sense of how the group will operate, feel like they have a part to play in it, and be poised for greater engagement. But if you squash member contributions and initial conflict, your group members will either leave the group or sit passively on the sidelines—and your group's development will be squelched. If you see that happening, look for ways to step back and invite others to step forward—even if it produces awkward conflict. This is essential.

STAGE 3: BUILDING RELATIONAL TRUST AND A WORKING STRUCTURE

When your group successfully works through the conflict that emerges in Stage 2, you will further establish the structure for how to work together *and* learn that you can duke it out and still maintain relationships. Trust begins to build, which begets *more sharing, more vulnerability*, and *more contributions*. Successful conflict resolution fuels your group's progress toward and movement into a third stage of development: *Trust and Structure*. And you begin to near Stage 4, the promised land.

Stage 3 bridges the awkward conflict of Stage 2 and the beautiful, integrated coordination and communication that characterizes

Stage 4. The goals of Stage 3 are to refine the group's purpose, goals, and ways of functioning, cultivate a group culture, and solidify trusting and engaged relationships.

Here are a few things you'll want to do as a leader to keep the development moving in Stage 3.

DANCE WITH YOUR GROUP MEMBERS.

We're not talking about literal dancing, but almost. This might feel as awkward as your first middle school dance, but embrace the moment and learn how to dance with your group. In Stage 1, the entire group was looking to you for guidance and direction, but as the group progresses, it's essential that you step back a bit and allow members to step forward and take on more ownership of the group, even taking on leadership roles. This doesn't mean you completely turn over the reins of the group. Rather, it means you dance with them: you step back, they step forward. They step forward, you step back.

Perhaps this visual image will help.

DANCING FOR DEVELOPMENT

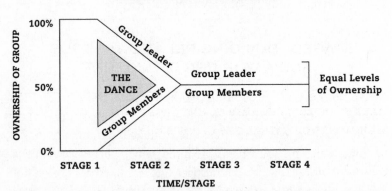

When a group first forms, all eyes are on the leader. Thus, the leader completely "owns" the group and its potential success. Over time, great leaders invite others to step forward and own more of the group. As group members step forward into ownership, great leaders graciously step back. This dance continues until everyone in the group—the leader(s) and members—owns the group equally.

To dance effectively, encourage and support your members' efforts to take on greater roles of responsibility and leadership. Whatever you do, your responsibility for doing all of the leading should decrease, while group members increase ownership of and within the group.

Building relational trust and a working structure will require you to make sense of conflict in a certain way. When you start to feel as if a member is stepping on your toes, you're typically not doing anything wrong. In fact, this probably indicates that you've done something right! As a member steps forward, secure and confident leaders willingly step back.

For instance, Courtney and her husband had been leading a group for about three years when one of the members interrupted her in the middle of a group and said, "You know, you used to give us some time to read and pray through the Scripture on our own after reading it aloud together and before discussing it. Do you think we could bring that back?" For a moment, it felt confrontational, but this was actually an indicator that things were moving in the right direction.

MAKE STRATEGIC CHANGES TO THE GROUP'S STRUCTURE TO FURTHER THE GROUP'S GOALS.

At this point, your group should have a greater understanding of its focus and goal. As the group leader, think about ways you could organize your group's meeting time, communication between meetings, meal planning, and so on to better facilitate reaching your goals. Instead of making executive decisions that you then impose on the group, bring ideas and suggestions to the group. Your group is now ready to figure out the best way to move forward together.

REFLECT WITH YOUR GROUP ON THE TRUST YOU'VE FORMED.
Contrary to popular opinion, relational trust is not a precursor to working well together. Instead, it emerges and grows *as* a group learns how to work well together. In other words, if the group has negotiated conflicts effectively and continues to prioritize group gatherings week after week, it's safe to say that your group members have come to trust one another and are leaning into deeper relationship with one another. Help your group to notice this, to reflect on and celebrate it, and to glean the important learnings that come from realizing this!

STAGE 4: ACCOMPLISHING YOUR GROUP'S PURPOSE TOGETHER

If Stage 3 goes well, your group members will be personally invested in and willing to actively contribute to the group's purpose, feeling like they can "work with" other members. They will take on important leadership functions, thereby increasing shared ownership of the group. Now your thriving group is ready to enter the group promised land. In Stage 4, termed *Work and Productivity*, your group focuses on doing what they are there to do and remains cohesive while encouraging challenging dialogue and transformational discipleship.

At this stage, everyone buys into the group's purpose and uniquely contributes to it. It's hard to distinguish the formal leader because leadership is shared among the group members. As a leader, you've done the hard work to get here, so you can now lean back in your comfy chair, focusing on and reminding members of the group's purpose, participating as an expert member of the group, and allowing people to fully contribute because you know the group can handle it.

This is where the magic happens. Members willingly open up and share because they trust one another and lovingly confront and speak truth because they are collectively committed to the group's purpose. Welcome to the promised land!

Unfortunately, getting to this point is not easy. Numerous small group studies suggest that only 20–25 percent of groups reach this golden stage of development.[2] At best, that's one in four, which means that for every four groups that start, three won't make it.

This explains why so many people have negative group experiences. They've never made it to Stage 4. The challenging conversations and struggles that are meant to be experienced, lived out, and overcome actually overtake a group, and its members are left wondering what could have been.

But this isn't a new problem. An entire generation of people and leaders, including the Israelites under the leadership of Moses, the most prolific Old Testament leader, missed out on the promised land. Their journey offers a good example of the messy life that happens within a community. Though the Israelites finally reached the promised land, they arrived much later than they'd hoped and under new leadership.

Without intentional leadership, your group will likely miss out on truly transformational group experiences. But by shifting your leadership mindset and understanding how to move your group through the stages, you can help your group enjoy the fruit of the promised land.

STAGE 5: ENDING YOUR GROUP AND BEGINNING ANOTHER

Reaching the promised land of group development will actually be the beginning of the end. Like a great movie trilogy or a book series, the pinnacle of your current group experience will begin the story of the next one. In Stage 5, often coined the "adjourning stage," your group will be *looking at what is next*. Groups do not remain in Stage 4 unless they experience continual changes that keep them focused.

Often, this means *launching* new leaders to start a group, *starting* a new small group yourself, or *establishing* a fresh new purpose to reinvigorate your group. Stage 5 presupposes healthy rhythms of leadership that encourage your own growth as you spur on others in their spiritual growth. The last three chapters of this book focus on the experiences you and your group will need to end and begin again.

I SEE WHERE WE'RE GOING, SO LET'S GO

Group development research provides a framework and roadmap to help leaders like you understand where you are and how to get where you want to go.

But getting there is going to require some shifts in your current thinking and behavior that can profoundly impact your group's experiences. No matter how short or long your group has been gathering, if you lead with the goal of reaching Stage 4 (or 5!), your group will be more apt to reach the promised land. Let's hit the road!

GUEST COMMENTARY

ACCELERATING COMMUNITY IN SHORT-TERM GROUPS

Danah and Brad Himes

Many groups are together for only 10–12 weeks. For instance, many college ministry groups operate on a semester schedule, and many groups meet over the short summer season. This creates a unique challenge for groups to thrive. However, during the short season in which they meet, members of short-term groups are ready and available for community. When they join a group, they are specifically looking to connect with peers while going deeper in friendship and faith. To meet these opportunities, leaders are trained to keep in mind the end goal of spiritual growth and community. By keeping this focus and putting in place a few intentional practices, leaders can set the pace towards an environment that fosters community and depth.

1. **Set the pace early.** When the group first forms, this is a vital time for the leader to set the pace and expectations. This can be done via an expectations sheet that includes details about the group, ground rules, and the study. The ground rules are very important and can include things such as: participation, attendance, confidentiality, and the vision of the group for the future. It is during this time that the leader sets the stage that the group is not there only for itself; rather, the vision of multiplication is cast, and the leader must periodically remind the group of its purpose.

2. **Prioritize time for sharing.** Whether through icebreakers, application questions, or the sharing of "highs and lows," leaders incorporate multiple "circle questions" into every week's gathering. Circle questions should be able to be answered by everyone and not necessarily have a right or wrong answer. By incorporating multiple circle questions beginning with the very first meeting, participation and sharing becomes the expectation.

3. **Model vulnerability.** Leaders must set the stage for both reflective sharing as well as being honest with their weaknesses. Too often, new leaders feel they need to prove that they have it all together. However, others will identify with them more in their weaknesses than in their strengths, leading to the cultivation of trust and depth.

4. **Connect individually.** Leaders get together with each member once outside the group context within the group's first few weeks of meeting. This practice allows members to be known personally by the leader and allows the leader to better know how to involve each one in the group. When a member experiences care, interest, and a leader's genuine faith and character, they are much more ready to open up and be more vulnerable with the rest of the group.

5. **Anticipate the ending.** Every group will end at some point, and the leader must lead through this delicate time. Even in one semester, relationships have formed, group members have shared joys and struggles, and transition can be difficult. Leaders must lean into closing well, leading the group to spend time reflecting on the group's journey and looking towards the future, and to celebrate important moments and relationships just as you would with other seasons of change (gather around a meal, have a picnic, etc.).

Whether you are involved in a college ministry or local church, when group members feel known and experience a group where all members share weekly, understand the direction of the group, and have a catalytic leader who sets the pace, groups can develop into thriving spiritual communities even in just a few weeks.

Danah Himes serves as associate campus minister at the Christian Campus House in Charleston, Illinois, where she oversees small groups. Brad Himes is the founder of The Groups Conference, working with churches in the areas of discipleship, groups, and leadership.

KEY TAKEAWAYS

1. Groups generally require a long time to become the kind where transformational growth occurs, but you can propel the process forward.
2. Your group needs dramatically different styles of leadership at various stages of its development, so resist taking a "one-size-fits-all" approach.

3. Early on, your group needs you to be a directive leader, then to gradually step back and allow others to step forward as the group develops. Remember to dance!
4. Trust develops when group members work together, including working through conflict. Allow the group to engage conflict and grow closer as a result.
5. Be patient and intentional as you lead your group through the typical developmental stages.
6. Reaching the promised land is both an ending and a beginning.

REFLECTION AND DISCUSSION QUESTIONS

1. **Remember:** What caught your attention in this chapter about group development?
2. **Understand:** How does group development theory explain group experiences you've had, both positive and negative?
3. **Apply:** Think about the last group you participated in or led. At which stage was the group when the group season/term ended?
4. **Apply:** Which stage do you think your small group is currently experiencing?
5. **Analyze:** What are ways you've seen group leaders effectively provide directive leadership as a group first forms?
6. **Evaluate:** If your group will only meet for a specific (and short) period of time, how can you adjust your expectations for what can and should be accomplished?

PART 2

FIVE SHIFTS TO TAKE YOUR GROUP TO THE NEXT LEVEL

To lead a thriving group, you'll need to help your group make these five shifts:

Chapter 4: Confused to Compelling:
Energize Your Group by Articulating Your Purpose

Chapter 5: Disengaged to Dedicated:
Set the Stage to Keep People Coming Back

Chapter 6: Mine to Ours:
Cultivate Commitment through Shared Ownership

Chapter 7: Trivial to Transformative:
Stimulate Meaningful Discussions

Chapter 8: Avoidance to Embrace:
Engage Difficult Conversations without Destroying Your Group

These chapters flesh out the *Leading Small Groups That Thrive* model, which will build your skill set to take your small group to the next level.

CHAPTER 4

CONFUSED TO COMPELLING

Energize Your Group by Articulating Your Purpose

Love does not consist in gazing at each other, but in looking outward together in the same direction.

—ANTOINE DE SAINT-EXUPÉRY

Several years ago, a large church asked Ryan to help their small groups move to the next level. He asked them to gather some quick feedback from their leaders by asking a few pointed questions, including this one: "What is the primary purpose of groups at your church?" While waiting for their responses, he sleuthed around the church's website and looked at their small groups ministry documents. The results were fascinating. There was almost no consistency in how church staff and group leaders articulated the purpose of their small groups:

- The small groups ministry website stated: "Our small groups go beyond just meeting and connecting together. They are the primary vehicles for living out the values we champion at Life

Church.[1] With this in mind, our desire is to create small groups that will be an irresistible witness to the community. We are committed to introducing people to groups, building up the body of Christ, networking groups to serve, preparing groups to go, and equipping facilitators to grow in their leadership."

- The leader application stated: "Life Church small groups, or 'L-Groups' for short, provide the optimal environment for the life-change Jesus Christ intends for every person."
- The leader guide stated: "The main thing is to keep the main thing the main thing—the primary goal is to build relationships that are guided by biblical principles."

When he visited them a few weeks later, Ryan asked, "So what is it? Life-change? Building relationships? Living out key values? Being an irresistible witness to the community?" He then explained that their core purpose couldn't be all of these things—each one requires a different focus and different strategies to accomplish it. You simply can't do it all with the same intensity.

Initially, the leadership team reacted defensively, but they soon softened. They couldn't believe they had been so unclear in explaining the purpose of their small groups, a major focus of their church.

We don't think they're alone.

Many problems groups experience are, at the core, problems of purpose. In groups, purpose problems are like structural and foundational issues in homes. You would never spend money remodeling a bathroom in a house that suffers from a crumbling foundation. You'd fix the structural issues first, and go from there. It's the same with groups. If you can get purpose right, you can build on that foundation. But if you suffer from purpose problems, you won't ever be able to move beyond them. Eventually, your group will crumble like a house built on sand, just as Jesus warned in Matthew 7.

In *Transformational Groups*, Ed Stetzer and Eric Geiger remind us that "groups need to be designed, considered carefully, and built with wise intentionality."[2] Purpose provides the structure and support necessary to withstand the onslaught of distractions and competing values groups encounter as they engage in the mess of human relationships. Purpose offers a firm foundation that reshapes the mess that inevitably occurs and turns it into opportunities for growth for everyone in the group.

Purpose is paramount. Here's what catalytic leaders know and do to get their purpose right and avoid a crumbling group down the road:

- Great leaders know their group can't be all things to all people.[3] This can result in a group becoming nearly nothing to only a few people.
- Great leaders are crystal-clear about and laser-focused on their purpose. If their purpose is relationship building, then everything leaders do is intended to reach that core goal. If it's discipleship, then they focus everything around following Jesus.
- Great leaders craft purpose in a way that connects with people's needs and greatest desires.
- Great leaders pursue a purpose that's about more than just the group itself.
- Great leaders continually remind their group of its mission and demonstrate how their group's purpose fits within the life and ministry of the overall church or organization.

CATALYTIC LEADERS *ARTICULATE PURPOSE*

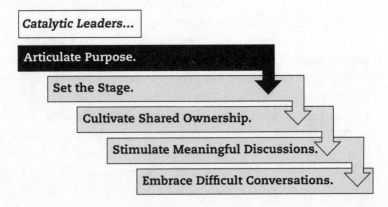

Catalytic Leaders...

Articulate Purpose.

Set the Stage.

Cultivate Shared Ownership.

Stimulate Meaningful Discussions.

Embrace Difficult Conversations.

In this chapter, we'll help you identify or clarify your group's purpose and articulate it in a way that energizes your small group.

IDENTIFYING YOUR PRIORITIES

Too many leaders underestimate the role purpose plays in offering direction for a group (or an entire ministry, for that matter). When asked to identify the top two or three priorities of their small groups ministries, pastors overwhelmingly named *fellowship* and *discipleship*, followed by *assimilation*. Small group leaders also named *fellowship*, *discipleship*, and *assimilation* as the most important.

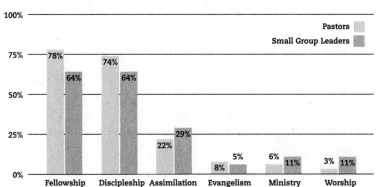

THE TOP PRIORITIES OF SMALL GROUPS

From the chart above, you can see that most small groups pastors and leaders agree that fellowship (relationships/community) and discipleship (spiritual growth) are the primary purposes of their small groups. But there's still a fairly significant gap—a 10–14 percent difference—between what pastors and what group leaders say are the primary purposes of small groups in their ministries. Are you curious what your group members think is the purpose of your small group?

So, who determines a group's purpose?

You, the leader, through conversation with group members.

If your group operates within a larger church or ministry, your purpose will be influenced by the organization's mission and its discipleship and connection strategy. As a leader, you must translate and contextualize the broader purpose of groups into a specific purpose for your particular group. Every group within a larger ministry should have its own unique purpose that falls within the broader mission of the small groups program.[4]

Groups that operate outside of a larger ministry umbrella should spend their first few meetings developing a shared sense of purpose and then revisit it regularly.

PRIORITIZING WITH THE GOAL OF SPIRITUAL GROWTH

Even though both pastors and small group leaders generally listed fellowship and discipleship as their top priorities, our data showed that groups that focused on other purposes demonstrated a greater contribution to spiritual growth. For instance, groups that prioritized ministry, evangelism, worship, and assimilation contributed more to their members' spiritual health than other groups. Oddly, groups that placed a relatively low priority on discipleship also contributed more to their members' spiritual growth.

What does this really mean?

It suggests that framing a group's purpose around those categories that are less frequently prioritized (ministry, worship, and evangelism) most affects individual spiritual growth. Thus, these priorities deserve greater emphasis than many leaders and pastors think, and they provide a more focused purpose.

Practically speaking, it seems as though groups that gather for the primary goals of building intentional relationships and growing in the Lord show smaller contributions to individuals' spiritual health. Perhaps this is because they generally require less effort. Groups that prioritize fellowship and discipleship may take the form of a book discussion, a shared meal, or simply rubbing shoulders with one another—all of which require minimal focus and preparation.

On the other hand, groups that prioritize discovering and using God-given gifts and talents (defined as ministry in our study) or surrendering one's heart and life to Christ on an ongoing basis (defined as worship) often require much more of group leaders and group members. Prioritizing a monthly rhythm of serving, praying with and/or caring for people outside the group on a regular basis, or pursuing ways group members can give sacrificially to God and his work are a few ways you can bolster spiritual growth. Groups with these priorities tend to require a great deal of preparation, focus, and intentionality in facilitating the group's time together.

The groups that prioritized something *other* than building relationships and growing spiritually actually showed the greatest spiritual growth.

Let's repeat that: the groups that prioritized something *other* than building relationships and growing spiritually actually showed the greatest spiritual growth. Now that's counterintuitive, isn't it?

But it doesn't surprise us. Eastview Christian Church, where Jason pastors, organizes their groups around four Gs: Gather, Grow, Give, and Go. But he's found that groups that focus on giving and going rather than gathering and growing are twice as likely to demonstrate growth and consistent gathering. Also, in Ryan's consulting work with leadership and ministry teams, he's found that groups that focus on driving organizational performance and hold themselves accountable for business results are more likely to actually build healthy, trusting relationships on the team.

We traditionally misunderstand how deep relationships form in community. Many well-intentioned leaders think you can achieve community by focusing on it. In reality, community tends to form when a group's members are not actually focusing on it. Growth and connection seem to be the by-products of other intentional purposes and practices.

OUTWARD FOCUS RESULTS IN COMMUNITY

Consider this: parents don't go to their kids' soccer practices and games to form community with other parents. They go to help their kids improve their soccer skills and grow into more well-rounded human beings. But in going to practices and games, coordinating travel arrangements, and shuttling kids all over the city, parents form meaningful connections and relationships with other parents.

The same is true for work teams. In *The Wisdom of Teams*, researcher-consultants Jon Katzenbach and Doug Smith explain that "a common, meaningful purpose sets the tone and aspiration" for any real team.[5] The pursuit of that purpose not only enables the team to achieve its goals, but to form a meaningful community characterized by trusting relationships. For instance, it's a well-known axiom among firefighters that nothing bonds like a fire. The dedicated pursuit of a common goal cultivates relationships, trust, and community.

Perhaps nowhere have we seen this dynamic more clearly than in the groups we've been in over the years. As mentioned in the preface, Ryan has shared life and friendship with six members of a discipleship group for over twenty years now. Only his wife knows him as well as the members of that group do. Even though they now live all over the country, those guys share more memories than any of them can count. But here's the deal. They do a low-grade, decent job of staying in touch throughout the year. Then, their connection and relationships get a serious boost every year when they start to plan for their annual trip. Choosing the date and location, coordinating logistics, assigning tasks, and doing everything required to make the trip happen puts them in a rhythm of contacting one another. The conversation quickly turns from flights and meal plans to discussions of marriage, the efforts and pitfalls of trying to be good dads, and the thorny issues they're all trying to navigate in their workplaces and families and churches.

The group understands this dynamic so well that they've articulated their purpose as a group not only for themselves, but for the people for whom their health, well-being, and continued spiritual growth matters most: their wives, children, colleagues, and friends. It's this externalized purpose that drives them deeper into community and intentional discipleship with one another. It's the same for your group, even if you don't know it yet.

Personal growth works the same way. After working with college kids for over two decades, Ryan recognized a common thread among many of the special, mature, and well-adjusted ones. They had all experienced something—a sibling with special needs, a grandparent living in their home, dedication to a mission serving others—that caused them to focus on someone other than themselves. In author Donald Miller's terms, they were drawn into a greater story, and they experienced great personal transformation along the way.[6]

This is exactly what happened to Linda, who leads a small group in a church on the East Coast. As she led her group, she recognized a growing dissatisfaction among her group members concerning how to genuinely live out their faith with people outside the group. They were learning about the need to evangelize but didn't know how to do it well. Thus, they made a concerted effort to redefine their group's purpose, changing it to learning how to become more missional.

Linda explained, "The group was pulling at me to help redefine how evangelism could be more relational." As the group redefined their purpose, they saw clarity and focus in their gatherings. "Our group's purpose became the force at every meeting. It was before us all the time—in our homework, in our meetings, in the Scripture we studied. Everything came back to the main purpose we had set for our group. Purpose became a constant mirror, unfolding itself every week." Their new purpose broke down the obstacles that were keeping them from living out the gospel in their everyday lives and gelling as a group.

Understanding this dynamic is especially important for men. Rarely are men attracted to a Saturday morning group focused on hanging out and building relationships. But give them a task to do—perform oil changes for single moms, paint a house for an elderly person, sync up a family cell phone plan, or fill a community's freezers with fresh elk meat—and they'll come in droves. Then, after the house is painted or the oil is changed, they'll gladly grab a burger to reward themselves for a good morning's work—and begin to cultivate community.

In *Small Groups for the Rest of Us*, Chris Surratt explains that his church's small group model is built on the trifold purpose of community, discipleship, and evangelism.[7] We suspect (and our study suggests) that the focus on evangelism might be what actually produces the community and discipleship they find in their groups.

Other churches follow a DNA group model. These groups engage:

Divine Truth (discipleship),
Nurturing Community (community and relationship), and
Apostolic Mission (evangelism and ministry)

Again, our data suggests the D and the N would be rendered fairly powerless without the third focus, A.

Ponds without water coming in or going out become stagnant. Groups without energy pouring into others suffer the same fate.[8] Make sure your pond doesn't grow stagnant. Ensure that your group's purpose includes an outward focus.

GETTING YOUR PURPOSE RIGHT

Whether your group is just starting out or has been together for many years, taking a look at your group's purpose will help you yield good fruit. Here are ten practical steps you can take to get purpose right for your group.

1. IF YOU'VE NEVER CLEARLY ARTICULATED YOUR GROUP'S PURPOSE, DO IT NOW.

It's never too late to define your group's purpose. As the saying goes, the best time to plant a tree was thirty years ago, but the next best time is *today*. If you've never clearly articulated your group's purpose, now is the time.

If your group is just starting out, it might make sense for you to take a lead role in articulating its purpose. Remember, when a group is new, members expect you to direct things and may feel uncomfortable contributing too much. However, if your group has been together for at least a few months, it is imperative that you do this *with* your group, and not on your own. In fact, if your group has been together for long enough that you've had some people come and go, consider reconnecting with those previous members and asking them about how purpose (or the lack thereof) played a role in their leaving. Use the Purpose Development Exercise provided on page 67 to get started.

2. CONSIDER AN OUTWARD-FACING PURPOSE, AND RESIST THE TEMPTATION TO MAKE IT ALL ABOUT YOU.

It's essential that the purpose of your group is not just about the members' comfort, relationships, and growth. Of course, the foundation of every ministry is the Great Commission—to go and make disciples. This means that discipleship is essentially a part of any group's purpose. But go beyond that to consider how your group can also focus on evangelism or ministry.

Remember, our study showed that groups that prioritized something other than building relationships and growing spiritually experienced the greatest spiritual growth. The effort your group shows toward reaching others will cultivate community within your group.

3. WHATEVER YOU DO, DON'T TELL PEOPLE THE PRIMARY PURPOSE OF YOUR GROUP IS SOLELY TO BUILD OR BE IN COMMUNITY.

Telling people your group's sole purpose is to build community might be the worst thing you could do. Decades of groups research has indicated that trusting relationships are a by-product of working together toward a goal—they are not the result of forced activities with the expressed purpose of getting to know each other. Yes, we realize this is counterintuitive, but it's true.

When Ryan worked with college students, leading residential life programs, his students would often explain that the purpose of their programming and services was to build community. He would typically retort, "Community for what?" Community is not an end in itself; rather, it is something God uses to mold us into the people he desires us to be and to make a powerful impact on the lives of others.

So, as you articulate your purpose with community in the headline, ensure that you answer the question, "Community for what?"

It's not wrong to tap into the felt need to belong (we talk more about felt needs in chapter 5). Everyone desires to be known. That felt need is real, but it's also elusive. Small groups ministries that focus on gathering for gathering's sake or community for community's sake will attract people initially, but they will likely not retain them for very long.

The reason for gathering must supersede the function of gathering.

One group member told us that when her family moved to a new city, they joined a group that eventually showed itself to be little more than a gathering with food and games that cost them more time and effort than they received. Ultimately, there's got to be more than surface-level friendship with people who happen to go to the same church.

Certainly, gathering is good (and biblical—think Hebrews 10), but we must remember that unless a gathering can produce a deeper experience, it won't be able to compete with the multitude of other options and better offers that will arise. The reason for gathering must supersede the function of gathering.

4. EXPLAIN TO YOUR GROUP THAT ACCOMPLISHING YOUR EXTERNALLY FOCUSED PURPOSE WILL ACHIEVE RELATIONAL DEPTH.

Don't worry! We're not all about outward action at the expense of close, trusting, personal relationships. Far from it. We value and enjoy close relationships with our small groups, and we're so grateful for them. We wouldn't trade them for anything.

Developing relationships in communities is why many people will actually show up to them in the first place. In fact, many folks join a small group in order to make new friends and develop relationships and community. But they won't stick around for just those things. Eventually, the communal benefits of the group will be overshadowed by busy work weeks, children's demanding schedules, and extra work at the office—and they'll stop coming.

Explain to your group members that they will achieve close community by pursuing the externally focused elements of your group's purpose.

5. ENSURE THAT YOUR GROUP POSSESSES A 5C PURPOSE.

In Ryan's previous book, *Teams That Thrive: Five Disciplines of Collaborative Church Leadership*, he presented a rubric to judge the quality of a team's purpose, which he called a "5C" purpose. We've adapted it for small groups. Great groups coalesce around a 5C purpose:

> **Clear:** How strongly does the group's purpose paint a clear picture of the group's value to members and potential members? Can everyone in your group easily explain why participating in the group is worth their time and energy?

Compelling: To what extent does the group's purpose address something that matters so much that members wouldn't miss a gathering unless they absolutely had to?

Challenging: To what extent is each member of the group required to meaningfully and consistently contribute to achieve the purpose?

Calling-oriented: How does accomplishing the group's purpose help members accomplish God's specific calling on their lives?

Consistently held: To what extent does every member understand the group's purpose, articulate it similarly, and pursue it consistently?

Once you and your group articulate your purpose, check in to ensure that it meets these 5Cs. If it doesn't, then keep working until you get to a place where your people agree that your group's purpose meets the 5C test.

6. ARTICULATE YOUR GROUP'S PURPOSE AS PART OF A GROUP COVENANT.

We don't want to get too formal here, but you really can't overemphasize your purpose. A group covenant is a great way to define relationships, commitments, and desired outcomes for your group. Remember, though, group covenants are not just a "one and done" moment; rather, you should reference the covenant often to drive the 5C concepts deep into your group's DNA. (We address group covenants more fully in chapter 5.)

7. INTRODUCE NEW PEOPLE TO YOUR GROUP'S PURPOSE.

Your purpose is the foundation of your group. When new members check out your group, take time to inform them of why you meet. Sara, a group leader from a large church in the Midwest, explained that taking visitors off to the side and explaining the group's purpose helps visitors gain perspective on the group. It also gives her a chance to detail what it means to be a part of the group. Doing this will also help you. Since everything should connect back to your purpose, articulating why you do what you do over and over will help you to live out that purpose in all you do.

8. CONSTANTLY REVIEW YOUR GROUP'S PURPOSE WITH YOUR GROUP.

On a regular basis, bring up the purpose of your group. This might feel awkward or like overkill, but it is so important. Brad, who leads a small group in the Midwest, told us that once a year, his group has a "Why are we doing this?" discussion. This conversation keeps purpose in the forefront of his group members' minds.

When Ryan gets together with his buddies for their annual trip, the first morning's task is to read and reflect upon the group's purpose. After pulling it up on Google Docs, they reflect on how they developed it over the years, ask if anything needs to change, and then carry on with the trip. It provides clear grounding for what they are seeking to accomplish during their days together.

TWO-MINUTE TIP

Remember those cards with group members' understanding of purpose? Individually rate the purpose statements they wrote out from 1 to 5 (5 being the highest) on each of the 5Cs. You'll quickly learn where your group's sense of purpose is both strongest and weakest, and then you can take steps to sharpen your group's purpose.

9. KEEP REMINDING YOUR GROUP ABOUT WHAT YOU ARE THERE FOR IN EVERY MEETING AND GATHERING.

It might become awkward, but there is great power in remembering. So keep reminding. Here are several easy ways to do that:

- At each meeting, ask a different person to state your group's purpose.

- As a group, recite your purpose together at the beginning of each meeting.
- Include your group's purpose in every email, every handout, every document you can to keep it in front of people.
- When you talk with people outside your group, share your purpose and what you love about your group.
- Include your purpose in text reminders of meeting times and locations.
- Share stories of times when your purpose has been accomplished/furthered in your group.

10. IF YOUR GROUP IS STRUGGLING, CONSIDER THAT THE PROBLEMS YOUR GROUP IS FACING MIGHT BE PURPOSE PROBLEMS.

Like any meaningful relationship, it's only a matter of time until your group will encounter some type of struggle. At the beginning of this chapter, we said that many group problems masquerade as people, trust, or relational problems when they are really purpose problems. What problem is your group struggling with? Inconsistent or lacking attendance? Lack of growth in community or as disciples? Superficial conversations that never get to the heart of the matter?

Certainly, groups can struggle for multiple reasons simultaneously. For example, inconsistent attendance could be a sign of a group member's overcommitment and unwillingness to prioritize the small group. It could be a sign of a potential interpersonal conflict or an undesirable curriculum selection. It could mean they have an allergy to something in the host's home and don't feel comfortable sharing that. Or it could be for an entire slew of other reasons.

Most likely there's a purpose problem embedded beneath those issues. Commitment is rarely a time-management issue, but a matter of competing values. When someone really wants to be a part of and contribute to a group, that person will find a way to attend, whether that means addressing and resolving a conflict or suggesting a change to the curriculum or meeting place.

Look for purpose problems at the root of many issues you'll be presented with as a leader. Recognize them as such and then deal with the root of the issue rather than simply the symptom. When you see problems, take some time on your own to see if you can identify the working purpose of your group. Ask yourself how your group members would explain the purpose of the group. Be honest. Don't fall into the temptation of sugar-coating or identifying what you hope they would say. Then, judge that purpose statement against the 5C framework. What's missing? What can you learn about what's wrong with your group's purpose? Use the Purpose Development Exercise to realistically and honestly ask tough questions and develop a refreshed purpose for your group.

GET TO WORK DEVELOPING YOUR PURPOSE

Are you ready to build a clear and compelling purpose that energizes and focuses your group?

TOOLS OF THE TRADE

PURPOSE DEVELOPMENT EXERCISE

1. My church/ministry says the purpose(s) of my small group is/are . . .
2. Based on what I've learned above, I could sharpen or strengthen the purpose of my group by (this is a good time to remember the 5Cs) . . .
3. If our group became all I could imagine it could be, the people most likely to benefit are . . .
4. I'm pretty sure that the people in (or who will join) my group are most interested in . . .
5. Take a shot at articulating an energizing group purpose.

Follow this simple, five-step process (by yourself or with your group) to develop a purpose that will build a foundation for success and growth in your group. The Purpose Development Exercise will be helpful as you work through this process.

First, find out what your church/ministry says is the purpose of small groups. Some of you are lone rangers, but most of you are part of a church, college, or ministry program. Consider what your organization says groups are all about, and think about how groups fit into your organization's wider disciple-making strategy.[9] Knowing what other programs are accomplishing may help narrow your group's purpose.

Second, evaluate the strengths and weaknesses of that broad purpose. Think about how you could sharpen, strengthen, or better articulate the purpose for your group.

Third, identify the external (outside of your group) beneficiaries of your group's community, spiritual growth, activities, etc. You've got to be thinking about an external focus for your group—that way it's not all about you. Who would benefit from your group if your group was amazing? For example, if you're doing a couples' early marriage group, the beneficiaries are those couples' kids and future kids, other couples they're friends with, and any couples they might mentor along the way. Or, if you're doing a men's group, people who stand to benefit from their growth and community would be their wives, children, employees, and coworkers. Another way to examine external impact is to honestly identify who or what outside your group would be negatively impacted if your group stopped meeting.

Fourth, explore the felt needs of your (potential) members. Realize here that many people aren't expressly looking to benefit others. They're looking for friends; they're trying to get past hang-ups and challenges; they're wanting to grow in a relationship with Jesus. Or maybe they're simply looking to do something on Thursday nights other than watch *Parks and Rec* reruns.

Keep in mind that previous research[10] found people who attend small groups most desire encouragement and acceptance, and those who don't attend most want encouragement and support. Everyone needs encouragement.

As the leader, you need to discover the needs of your group! While this might be hard work now, it will pay huge dividends as your group forms and begins to meet.

Finally, take a shot at articulating your purpose. Do this in a way that connects those felt needs (#4) with a ministry focus (#3). Be creative. Give yourself some time. Play with it.

We suggest you tackle Steps 3–5 at your first or second group meeting, though you could also do it on your own. Here are some sample purpose statements that tie together all the elements we discuss in this chapter:

> *Growing a community of Jesus followers who seek to shine the light of Jesus to our neighbors and coworkers.*
>
> *Becoming the people God designed us to be for our good and for the good of our community.*
>
> *Loving each other in mutually challenging relationships to make God known in our city.*
>
> *Gathering together as Christ followers in order to learn how to love, serve, and influence those around us.*
>
> *More and deeper disciples making more and deeper disciples for God's glory and his mission.*

If you did this exercise by yourself, please do not present the purpose statement you've developed to your group as a finished product. Instead, introduce it to your group at your first meeting and allow them to comment on it, critique it, and together make it better. Remember, you can use the 5Cs to judge whether or not your purpose statement will be one that will engage and energize your group! (We talk more about shared ownership in chapter 6.)

PUTTING YOUR PURPOSE INTO PRACTICE

Congratulations! You've taken a huge step in framing your purpose. Remember that everything you do from here on out should be based on what will help your group to best pursue your unique purpose rather than on what you or your church has always done, or what you most enjoy or think is most convenient. **Everything hinges on your purpose and should be determined by your purpose.**

The next chapter will help you put your purpose into practice, no matter what season your small group is in.

THE POWER OF ALIGNING YOUR CHURCH'S MISSION AND SMALL GROUP VALUES

Dave Ferguson

Standing in front of a large group of people at Community Christian Church, Brian told a story about a dark time when he was not only far from God, but sure there was no God. As Brian talked, he chronicled all the painful ways he tried to find love and purpose, which never satisfied him. Then he described how his friend invited him to a small group. Brian paused, then said with emotion, "That community group saved my life." In that group, Brian discovered unconditional love and a purpose for his life, and found his way back to God.

I could feel my heart beating fast as everyone applauded Brian's courage. "This is why I do what I do," I thought. My life passion is to help people find their way back to God. It's why I started a church. It's why I help plant churches. And it's why I write books. Everything I do comes back to the mission of helping people find their way back to God.

So it's not surprising that the mission at Community Christian Church, where I serve as lead pastor, is to "Help people find their way back to God." Brian was a great example of how our small groups play a vital role in accomplishing our mission. People find their way back to God when they get connected to life-giving community. Here's how our three small group values contribute to our church's overall mission.

Community Groups Connect the Unconnected

We all need relationships with others who can encourage us and help us through the ups and downs of life. A small group is where people experience genuine community. The relationships we develop in small groups become the relationships that will get us through anything. I remember one small group where the husband of one of the couples was diagnosed with cancer, which meant regular treatments. The small group stepped up and babysat the kids, made hospital visits, prepared meals for the family, and on and on. The small group had become like family. Within a year, the husband passed away, and at the funeral his wife said, "I never could have gotten through this time without my small group." That's what small groups are about: connecting the unconnected and helping provide care through whatever life throws at you.

Community Groups Develop 3C Christ-Followers

Small groups are also places where people grow spiritually and in their relationship with Jesus. A 3C Christ-follower is someone who celebrates their relationship with God every day and gathers weekly to praise God and yield their life more fully to him. They connect with other Christ-followers, which God uses to grow them in Christlikeness. Finally, 3C Christ-followers contribute their time, talents, and resources to further the mission of Jesus in our communities and world.

In our groups, these purposes are fulfilled in multiple ways. We ask our leaders to facilitate their meetings by leading a discussion centered around the Sunday morning messages. Over time, this creates a safe environment where people can share how the truth of the weekly messages relates to the reality of their lives. In this way, the leader and the group members are supporting and challenging one another to grow as Christ-followers. We also ask leaders to challenge their groups to serve on one of our ministry teams. We encourage our people to serve outside the church by asking how they can bless their neighbors, coworkers, and other people in their circle of influence. So small groups might serve at homeless shelters, throw block parties in their neighborhoods, or even adopt refugee families through organizations like World

Relief. To those ends, we coach and resource our leaders to help our people grow as 3C Christ-followers.

Community Groups Develop, Reproduce, and Deploy Leaders

We ask every small group leader to identify and train up what we call an apprentice leader. We've found that groups provide an optimal context for leadership development. Hundreds of leaders grow into their leadership callings as they take on greater responsibility over time through the five steps of leadership development (explained in chapter 10 of this book).

We need all these elements of church life. There's no way we could accomplish our mission of "helping people find their way back to God" without small groups. The way groups connect people, develop Christian maturity, and develop leaders is essential to our spiritual growth and the growth and reproduction of our church. Know the mission of your church or ministry, and allow your small groups to play a key role in accomplishing that mission.

Dave Ferguson is the lead pastor of Community Christian Church, visionary for the international church-planting movement NewThing, and president of the Exponential Conference. Connect at DaveFerguson.org.

KEY TAKEAWAYS: HOW TO SHIFT FROM *CONFUSED TO COMPELLING* IN DIFFERENT GROUP SEASONS

WHEN LAUNCHING A NEW GROUP

1. Use the 5 Cs to create and define the purpose of groups for your church or ministry.
2. In light of the church vision for groups, ask members why they joined this group at this time.
3. Work with your group to establish how your group will specifically and uniquely focus on that purpose in your group.
4. Establish a group covenant that highlights your purpose and how you will pursue it.

WHEN MAINTAINING YOUR GROUP'S MOMENTUM AND EFFECTIVENESS
1. Take stock of how your group members talk about your group's purpose and collaboratively articulate it using the 5Cs.
2. Ask your group how well it is doing at (a) focusing on that purpose, and (b) accomplishing that purpose. Then identify 2–3 ways your group can do better.
3. Remind them of your group's purpose every week (collaboratively developed by them!). This may mean reminding them of the group covenant to which they've agreed.

WHEN YOUR GROUP IS STRUGGLING
1. Remind your group of its purpose when it began.
2. Ask members to determine their continued commitment. Give an "out" for any group member(s) who would like to/need to leave.
3. Release any leaders ready to start a new group.
4. Renew the group around a revitalized purpose using the Purpose Development Worksheet.
5. Recruit new members who may align well with the newly formed purpose.

REFLECTION AND DISCUSSION QUESTIONS

1. **Remember:** What caught your attention in this chapter?
2. **Understand:** What do you now understand about the relationship between an outward-facing purpose and inward-focused community?
3. **Apply:** What words or phrases come to mind when you think about the purpose of the group you're currently leading?
4. **Analyze:** Think about the problems you've experienced in groups you've been a part of in the past. How could you reframe those problems as purpose problems?
5. **Evaluate:** How might problems related to your group's purpose be related to the problems you're experiencing in leading the group?
6. **Evaluate:** Think about a recent experience that galvanized your group. What did you do? Was the goal at the onset to grow together or was the closeness of your group a by-product? What's the next experience your group could engage in to help you grow closer together?
7. **Create:** If you were to draft a new 5C purpose for your small group, what would you want it to be?

CHAPTER 5

DISENGAGED TO DEDICATED

Set the Stage to Keep People Coming Back

Who wants to sail on a skipperless ship?

—PRIYA PARKER

Have you ever been part of a conversation like this?

> **Group Leader:** Hey, I think my small group is done.
> **Small Groups Pastor:** Jim, oh no! Last time we talked, you thought it was going well. What's going on?
> **Group Leader:** I don't know what happened. We started out well a few months ago, and everyone seemed excited to meet, but for some reason, no one was able to meet for our last two gatherings. I feel like we've been fizzling for a while. I'm not sure what to do.

Sound familiar?

Pam shows up two weeks in a row, then never comes back. Victor asks questions at the group sign-up table, but never fills out the online form. Bill, Jan, Kezziah, and Joseph all come to a couple of meetings and say they're going to commit. But when week three rolls around, they're nowhere to be found.

If you're like us, you've experienced various failed attempts to gather people into your group and to develop a sense of place that keeps them coming back. Each of these scenarios is a result of problems with one or both of the following things: the motivation to fully engage in a group, and the predictability and safety offered by a group's structure. You might think of structure as the walls that are built upon the foundation of purpose.

Once you know why your group exists, you, as a catalytic leader, must set the stage for transformational group experiences by building a solid structure that gives the group what it needs to grow into a healthy community where members are committed to doing life and growing spiritually together. You'll need to leverage your group's size; gather the right people, who can benefit from your group's experience; structure group gatherings to support your group's purpose; and encourage psychological safety among the group. If you do these things, your group will become a space where devoted people can grow and pursue their unique purpose together.

CATALYTIC LEADERS *SET THE STAGE*

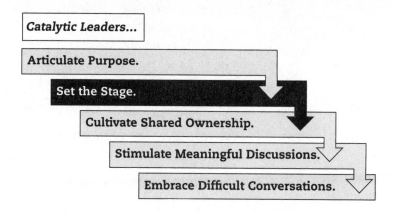

Catalytic Leaders...

Articulate Purpose.

Set the Stage.

Cultivate Shared Ownership.

Stimulate Meaningful Discussions.

Embrace Difficult Conversations.

The equation below illustrates how you can get off to a good start and begin to build a transformational community:

Stimulus + Structure = Set the Stage for Growth

When people are properly motivated to join and engage your group (the stimulus), then find a plan and predictable ways to interact when the group first begins (the structure), they experience psychological and relational safety that yields opportunities to contribute to the group and begin a group journey toward growth (set the stage for growth). By attending to these issues, you can create a safe space that keeps people not only coming back but wanting to dive deeper into community and growth. This chapter will help you cultivate a dedicated group that keeps coming back for more.

STIMULUS: GATHERING YOUR GROUP WITH PURPOSE

Recently, Ryan saw a huge banner hanging on a traditional church building. It beckoned, "Are You Looking for Community?" This church was marketing itself as a place to find community, but we doubt that being in community was the church's actual mission or purpose. That church is hedging its bets that seeking community is a gateway for people to come to the church and join its mission of making disciples.

In the previous chapter, we discussed the relationship between a person's motivation for joining a group and the group's purpose. But here's the tricky part: the group purpose you've articulated may not initially compel people to join your group. In other words, your group's *why* may not initially match why people want to join.

UNDERSTAND WHY PEOPLE WOULD WANT TO JOIN A GROUP

Understanding what people are looking for will help you know how to market your group. Why would potential members want to join *a* group? Why would potential members want to join *your* group? You'll need to think about the population you wish to engage and then become experts on these folks: what drives them, what they need, what's missing in their lives, and more.

If you can figure that out, you'll have a better shot at selling your group and getting people to come and be ready to engage.

Do the new people in your church need friends, or do they need to find a way to step further into the rhythm of the church? Are people fed up with their sin and looking for a way to stop doing the same things over and over? Are people looking for something to do on the weekends? Are people looking for a place to serve in their community? What are they looking for?

A good place to start is to consider your own *why*. Why did *you* join a small group in the first place, let alone agree to lead a small group? If you explore that, you'll discover that your needs probably aren't that different from others'.

From there, you need to connect people's reasons for joining a group to your group's actual purpose.

CONNECT THEIR WHY TO YOUR GROUP'S WHY

You can connect their motivation for joining your group's purpose by employing some small behavioral encouragements, as is customary in the marketing world. For instance, years ago, a grocery store placed pointed arrows on the floor leading to the produce section. Properly nudged, people followed these arrows, and produce sales skyrocketed. Noted behavioral economist Richard Thaler calls these little manipulations of behavior "nudges." Nudges alter "people's behavior in a predictable way without forbidding any options or significantly changing their economic incentives . . . Nudges are not mandates. Putting the fruit at eye level counts as a nudge. Banning junk food does not."[1]

Nudges can move us in small ways to make better choices. This is why health promoters urge you to keep fatty snacks on a higher shelf in your cupboard or set out your exercise gear the night before an early morning workout. There's nothing inherently valuable about setting out your clothes, keeping Doritos on the top shelf, or turning right at the arrow—but doing these things helps us to get more of the behaviors we really want.

In our case, we want to nudge people to grow spiritually and invest in the sanctifying work of Jesus by joining a small group. But we also know that most people join for other reasons—reasons like "community." The promise of belonging in community can be the nudge they need to invest in their spiritual growth.

Northcoast Church in Southern California noticed that people new to the church lack established relationships and seek more connection, but they don't want to impose on those who are already connected. So they put new people into new groups. Those people share a need for greater connection (their reason for joining) and have room in their lives for more relationships; they can then connect in an environment where spiritual growth can occur (your actual group purpose).[2]

When you gather your group, make it explicit to potential members that your group can give them what they *want* (their motivation for joining), and also what they *need* (your group purpose).

INVITE WITH INTENTIONALITY

Imagine what would happen if a local business simply set up shop and waited for people to patronize it. That's not a great business model. At best, they'd wait months for the word of mouth approach to drum up business.

But this is what too many leaders do. Leaders may ensure that their contact information and group description are included on the church website, but then they sit and wait.

What if you—with your group's hopeful purpose in mind—personally invited people to join your group? Imagine how powerful it would be to tap the shoulder of someone who is disengaged from the church or someone who is seeking friendship and discipleship. What if that person has been waiting for your invitation?

In many situations, the best invitation is a personal one. Why not also in the church? Likely, the more intentional you and your existing group members are about directly inviting new people, the more you will find success in gathering your group and stimulating group growth.

Organic, everyday connections with people around you produce a ripe field for invitations. See a host of tips on how to create these connections in Chris Surratt's guest commentary at the end of this chapter. But, then, as you consider personally recruiting your group, reflect on these helpful suggestions from Bill Search's *The Essential Guide for Small Group Leaders*[3]:

> **Pray.** Ask the Holy Spirit to be the foundation for this group.
>
> **Be open-minded.** Don't think of the "usual" suspects. Step back and literally look around. Think through your interactions over the last month or two and consider who might be interested in joining you.
>
> **Make a list.** Write down every name that comes to mind (without editing along the way).
>
> **Invite.** Be bold. Ask a trusted person to hold you accountable to invite everyone on your list by a certain date.
>
> **Be clear.** Invite people to a time and place, and give them a good reason why they should come. Remember to tap into their felt needs and your compelling purpose.

TWO-MINUTE TIP

Who comes to mind? Who has God recently put in your path? Is there a group of friends who already enjoy each other and may want to engage in a deeper purpose together? Who do your current group members rub shoulders with on a regular basis that aren't already in a small group? In two minutes, quickly write their names in the margin.

STRUCTURE: CULTIVATING PREDICTABLE ENVIRONMENTS

Everyone appreciates predictability, especially when joining a new group or starting a new group session. But too few group leaders take this into account when designing initial meetings. Structures provide the predictability that so many people desire, especially in the initial stages of group formation.

Your group members want to know what time to be where, what they can expect from you as the leader and from others in the group, and how they will fit in. These structures will breed the psychological and relational safety that will enable your group to go deep and experience personal and spiritual growth.

DETERMINE YOUR OPTIMAL GROUP SIZE

Very simply, group size matters a lot.

When Matt and Courtney were first approached to lead a small group at our church, they lived in a three-story, two-bedroom condo. They knew that the church limited groups to twenty, but they also knew two things: (1) They didn't have more than eight chairs and a couch, and (2) twenty was way too big for their purpose. So they asked if their group could be limited to a maximum of ten or twelve.

What is the optimal size for *your* small group?

Carl George, a small group pioneer, has often been quoted as saying, "Everyone needs to be cared for by someone, but no one can take care of more than about ten." In our study, the smaller the group, the more the group contributed to individuals' spiritual health. In addition to asking leaders how many people were in their group, we

Groups that had fewer than eight core members or more than seventeen core members showed the greatest influence on members' spiritual growth.

also asked them how many group members attended at least three out of four group gatherings. These are the people we refer to as "*core members*." Groups that had fewer than eight core members or more than seventeen core members showed the greatest influence on members' spiritual growth. We think there are at least two reasons for that effect.

The first reason is that smaller groups are able to reach a level of intimacy and task effectiveness that is really difficult to accomplish in larger groups. In fact, author and pastor Greg Ogden argues that the optimal discipleship group should be three people.[4] Members in smaller groups are able to engage in ways that are much more difficult for larger groups. They can share detailed stories that allow them to get to know each other well. They each get a lot of floor time and don't have to compete with many others to get a word in.

Many studies suggest that the ideal size for groups is 5–9 members. A group of this size is big enough to benefit from the diversity of the various members, but small enough to easily coordinate their work and stay connected as one group without splitting into sub-groups. For instance, the group Sherry leads has seven core members, and this size allows each person to fully invest in the group. The smaller size creates enough space for each person to share their joys and sorrows, and this has created a strong family feel in the group.

The second reason is that larger groups may split into subgroups, which allows them to enjoy the greater intimacy and task effectiveness of smaller, more intimate groups. Group leaders might split a larger group into smaller groups for prayer or discussion. To do so, the leader must identify additional leaders in the group to coordinate the smaller groups. For instance, Marv's group consists of twenty-four members (nineteen are core members). They meet together as a large group to connect and to have an overview of the sermon study, then he splits the large group into two subgroups in the same home. He has raised three other leaders to help facilitate both groups. This strategy allows for each subgroup to maximize its discussion and structures each group for good interaction.

An additional reason is related to the group's external purpose (as discussed in chapter 4). Larger groups have more people power to leverage, prompting broader ministry efforts that push the group to higher levels of connection and purpose. When these things happen, it's no surprise that large groups continue to flourish.

So we've got thriving small groups, and we've got thriving large groups. Then there's this no-man's land in the middle.

When groups have somewhere between 10–15 core members, discussions with the whole group may not yield great participation or engagement. Leaders may not recognize how large the group actually is, so they don't break out into smaller groupings. Our data suggests that leaders realize they need to create more intimate settings when their group is somewhere around seventeen members.

So what size should your group be? We suggest keeping it small. Whether you get there by keeping the entire group small or by splitting your large group into smaller subgroups for part of your gathering time, a smaller group size will ultimately allow your group members to achieve greater intimacy and spiritual growth.

Whatever you do, play an active role in determining your group's size. Be decisive. Your decision will most certainly affect your members' engagement and potential spiritual growth.

DETERMINE YOUR MEETING FREQUENCY

While you'll likely consider your own schedule and preferences, you should also consider the schedules of your target demographic. Think about when they'll be most vibrant and alive. Perhaps a post-college young professionals group might meet for dinner and discussion around 6:30 p.m. on a weeknight. A young families' group, on the other hand, might meet at 4 or 5 p.m. on a weekend to accommodate the little ones' bedtime. Schedule your group around *who* you want there.

Then, plan to meet regularly.

When it comes to determining meeting times and locations, balance what will help accomplish your group's purpose with what is feasible for the members of your group. That likely will create tension—accommodating toddler Emily's 7:30 bedtime might make it difficult to meet long enough to get into rich discussion. Emphasizing convenience over purpose might result in an ineffective and passionless group, but prioritizing purpose over the realities of family life and other commitments might result in a group that can never meet all together—and for the record, groups that don't meet don't see any spiritual growth in their members!

Seventy-five percent of the groups in our study met on a weekly basis. That's a good thing, according to our data, because the more time the group spends together, the more the group contributes positively to its members' spiritual growth. In our study, groups contributed more to members' spiritual growth when they met at least weekly (as opposed to every other week or even less often).

One of the reasons weekly gatherings are so important is because group members will likely miss a meeting occasionally. When a member skips or misses an every-other-week gathering, you may not interact with that group member for a month or longer. Absences like that don't exactly spur growth in community and discipleship.

Once you've determined a schedule that works for you and your group members, it's important that you meet when you say you're going to meet—no matter what. If you say you're going to meet weekly, then do that. You'll be tempted to cancel if only three or four group members can attend. You'll be tempted to cancel if you've had a busy week and haven't had time to prepare as well as you would like. Fight those temptations.

If you cancel a group gathering because fewer group members are available that night, you'll create uncertainty for your group members. They'll no longer be sure whether the group will meet on any given week. Unpredictability doesn't yield safe environments for group members to invest in one another and grow spiritually. Invite the Lord to meet you in the intimacy that a smaller group affords and affirm for all members, present or not, that your group gathering is something on which they can depend.

Josh, a small group leader on the West Coast, encourages leaders and members to keep showing up: "That's the biggest thing. We try to be there as much as we possibly can. A lot of times, we are just there, and we are real. We may not always be super prepared, but we're always there."

SELECT THE RIGHT VENUE

Where's the best place to meet—a coffee shop, someone's home, at church?

"Venues are a type of nudge,"[5] argues Priya Parker, author of *The Art of Gathering.* The place you meet sets the stage for what you can accomplish during your meeting. So be *really* strategic.

The purpose of your group must determine the location in which it most often gathers. If your group's purpose is evangelistic in nature, consider meeting in a public space, such as a coffee shop or a member's front yard, where others can notice your group. If your group is intended to provide accountability in members' private lives, choose a private place where people can share without risk of being overheard. If your purpose involves discerning your spiritual gifts and engaging effectively in vocationally diverse mission fields, consider a comfortable discussion space such as a living room.

Belle's small group gathers at a local fitness center. After engaging in a workout class together, her group meets in the cafe area for their weekly group time. Because their group's purpose includes evangelism, they strategically set out a few extra chairs so that anyone from the fitness class can join them. The strategic location and extra chairs have resulted in several new members joining the group.

As you consider different locations, remember that it can be beneficial to change the location from time to time. If you typically meet in a home, what outside-the-home experiences could help your group accomplish your purpose? If you meet in a public space, how could meeting in a private space occasionally enrich your group?

DECIDE HOW LONG TO MEET

The average duration of small group gatherings in our study was one hour and fifty minutes. However, the most thriving groups gathered for at least two hours and fifteen minutes per week. You might wonder, *What's so magical about twenty-five more minutes?* That additional time allows group members to take their time getting into the meat of their gathering time. It allows group members to relax as they spend time engaging and building community. It also gives them more time to deal with logistics.

Ultimately, leaders of thriving groups know the importance of asking the questions above and then carefully crafting their frequency, location, and duration based on the group's purpose, knowing that the right combination of these exponentially increases its effectiveness.

TWO-MINUTE TIP

Take a sheet of paper, and draw out the ideal seating setup within the ideal setting that will help your group thrive. Then, compare that to your current group meetings. Does your current location fit your purpose? Do you meet frequently enough for your group members to interact regularly? Does your group have enough time to thrive?

INTENTIONALLY STRUCTURE YOUR TIME

We've established that groups that thrive try to meet for at least two hours and fifteen minutes. Now, what will you do with that time? How you divvy it up depends greatly on your group's purpose. As with everything else, let your purpose drive the structure of your group time. In the following paragraphs, we'll share some data with you that might help you as you think about your meeting's structure.

Study

On average, groups spent 75 percent of their time in discussion, Bible study, or both. And that's not surprising. But what is surprising is that the amount of time devoted to small group discussion and Bible study did not contribute significantly to members' spiritual growth. This leads to two important questions:

1. What *does* contribute to members' spiritual growth?
2. Why doesn't discussion and Bible study contribute to members' spiritual growth?

As we explained in chapter 4, purposes other than discipleship and fellowship spurred greater growth in individual members' spiritual health. Yet groups spend the majority of their time engaging in discussion and Bible study. We certainly don't advocate that you entirely eliminate this time. But we do want you to consider why this time might not contribute to growth as much as other activities.

One factor may be that group discussion and Bible study often contribute to the *maintenance* of a person's faith, but it may not contribute to that person's spiritual *growth*. For the record, that's OK! Certainly not every small group gathering is meant to be a life-changing, mountain-top spiritual experience. We encourage you to continue to spend time in the Word of God—just be aware that being in the Word of God together may not yield the greatest value in exchange for your time together.

Another contributing factor may be that, more often than not, leaders are not trained to effectively lead group discussions. If you want group discussions to be a main component of your group time, and to contribute to members' spiritual growth, you'll need to take some precautions to ensure your discussions have the desired impact. You'll need to strengthen your ability to ask great questions, design your space for maximum impact, and facilitate fantastic conversations (more on this in chapter 7).

Worship

Our data suggests that the most effective groups spend a greater-than-average amount of time in worship. On average, the groups we surveyed spent five minutes in worship. In comparison, the most effective groups spent about fifteen minutes in worship—which was about 15–30 percent of their group time. Most groups did not worship together at all.

The most effective groups spent about fifteen minutes in worship.

There's a lot of research out there suggesting that singing together unifies a group.[6] Our study seems to affirm this. The more a group worships together, the more the group contributes to members' spiritual growth.

Logistics

While many groups reported that they spent no time at all on logistics, the most effective groups in our study typically spent more than twelve minutes of each meeting dealing with logistics. That might seem like an odd thing to commit time to, but these groups were trying to do grand and complicated things—the kinds of things that reflect an outward-facing purpose and build intimacy in groups. They needed sufficient time to deliberate and make plans.

How can you incorporate logistical discussions into your group? Well, don't spend twelve minutes figuring out who's bringing dinner next week. That's torture. Instead, spend time discussing how your group can accomplish ministry. Brainstorm how to support a local missionary, how to serve in your community, what to include in the care packages you're sending abroad. Spend time coordinating a fundraiser for a local nonprofit, sharing updates on how to partner with church staff, or figuring out how to send meals to someone in the church body. A longer meeting time will accommodate these logistical discussions and make it so that your group doesn't need to rush through each meeting. Take the time to discuss and do the things that make a difference.

Prayer

We were surprised to discover that the more time the group spends in prayer, the less the group contributes to its members' spiritual growth. It seems counterintuitive, doesn't it? Shouldn't spending lots of time praying together lead to greater spiritual growth? Our data says no—at least not during group gatherings.

While groups spent an average of thirteen minutes in prayer, the groups that contributed the least to members' spiritual health spent more than twenty-one minutes in prayer. We wonder if perhaps these groups spent twenty minutes sharing prayer requests and twenty minutes praying together—altogether, a long time.

What should you do instead?

First, structure prayer around your group's purpose. Set expectations and limits, then use the time strategically. Missionally-minded groups could spend their time praying by name for specific people. Family-oriented groups could focus their prayer on one family per week and pray specifically for each member of that family. Maybe you start every group by asking one member these three questions:

- What will you be doing Thursday morning at 10 a.m.?
- What do you love about what you're doing?
- How can we pray for your place of work?

This interview format enables you to learn about members' individual mission fields—plumbers, accountants, artists, and stay-at-home parents alike. Then you can pray over their work in specific and succinct ways.

Second, creatively structure prayer around your group dynamics. Pair up members and ask them to share their prayer requests with one another and commit to pray for one another throughout the week. Invite members to communicate by phone, text, or email about those prayer requests throughout the week.

Strategically and creatively structuring your prayer time will permit you to leverage group prayer time for the good of the group. Too often, the individual-focused prayer requests we invite don't necessarily contribute to the group. Of course, these dynamics will vary for different groups. But we hope you'll think through what actually serves your group and avoid a prayer strategy that serves the individual to the detriment of the group.

GO AHEAD AND BREAK THE MOLD—THOUGHTFULLY

Every decision you make about how your group spends its time should be based on your group's purpose. Don't rely on tradition, previous practice, or convenience. Unfortunately, many leaders spend 2–3 minutes making these logistical and structural decisions for their groups, without much deliberation about the relative advantages and disadvantages. Don't do that. Think and strategize. Be an active participant in structuring your group, even as you are gathering it. Then, once your group comes together, be willing to make adjustments that will help your group achieve its unique purpose.

Remember the formula for launching your group successfully:

Stimulus + Structure = Set the Stage for Growth

By strategically planning your group's structure, you will help your members predict what is to come and be able to fully engage—and you'll create a safe and welcoming space for people to come, grow, and fully engage with the group. As you do, you'll move people from disengaged to dedicated.

PREPARING FOR AND HOSTING YOUR FIRST GROUP GATHERING

We'll close this chapter by helping you plan a killer first meeting, taking into account all that this chapter has presented. You've thought through the structure of your group, and now you're days away from your first group gathering. How do you reap the benefits of all of the decisions you've made?

Think back to Stages 1 and 2 of group development, which we detailed in chapter 3. Remember that when a group initially comes together (Stage 1: Inclusion and Dependency), group members are looking to their established leader to tell them what to do and make them feel comfortable. They're trying to figure out what constitutes acceptable behavior in the group. As a leader, you've got to provide this guidance. If you do it well, people will begin to feel comfortable, and the group will begin to debate and fight a bit about what they want to accomplish and how they want the group to go (Stage 2: Counterdependency and Conflict). When you start to see people pushing back and offering alternative suggestions, you'll know your group is moving forward.

What can you do to help your group members move through Stage 1 to Stage 2?

BEFORE YOUR FIRST GATHERING, CLEARLY COMMUNICATE YOUR PLAN.

When your group is first coming together, you'll have the opportunity to connect with members who express interest in your group.

These first interactions are a fantastic opportunity to work on setting the stage and building spaces for growth.

Your group doesn't start at the first meeting. It starts as soon as your group members learn about it from that glossy flyer or website listing. You set expectations early, so leverage these moments. Particularly when you have high expectations for your group and when members might be reluctant to offer their best to the group, you must prepare your group members to be able to contribute well. In a sense, you are priming them for a great group experience to which they significantly contribute.[7]

In your in-person, phone, email, and text conversations, let prospective members begin to understand the value of their engagement in your group. Help them understand that you have a plan of attack and that they can rely on your leadership. Help them understand that you care about who they are and will care for them in your group. Use the following checklist to help you make the most of your communication prior to your first meeting.

TOOLS OF THE TRADE

CHECKLIST FOR PRE-MEETING COMMUNICATION

☐ I've sent a personalized welcome note to every new member as soon as they joined that includes:
  ○ A statement about why we do our group
  ○ A plan for the first meeting (so that the new member feels comfortable)
  ○ What I expect from everyone at the first meeting
☐ I've asked an existing member of our group to reach out to each new person (if there's an existing group that new members are being added to).
☐ I've sent a reminder about the first meeting (a couple of days before the meeting) and expressed my excitement about it.
☐ I've taken the time to pray for each individual by name.

AT YOUR FIRST MEETING, IMPLEMENT YOUR PLAN.

If you've done the pre-meeting communication well, then your job at the first meeting is to make good on your promise.

Implement your plan. At the first few group gatherings, members won't be ready to decide on the group structure. It's like asking students on the first day of class to give a presentation on course content that same day. For most people, that's overwhelming. So lead your group and implement what you planned ahead of time. Give your group members an overview of how you'll spend your time at group gatherings, even if you've already done so in that pre-meeting email. If you share a meal or dessert together, lay out how the menu gets planned and how your meal system works. If you're studying a book together, distribute the books with a printed schedule that lists what you'll cover each week. If you've got kids or elders to care for, make a plan. Provide the structure that is so important for a group early on.

TOOLS OF THE TRADE

ACCOMMODATING CHILDCARE OR ELDERCARE

☐ Depending on your group's makeup, it's important to think through childcare and/or eldercare. When parents know their kids are cared for, they're more able to engage. When members know their elderly parents are cared for, they, too, are more able to engage. Taking some time to consider how you can serve your members' needs will allow them to be physically, mentally, and emotionally present.

☐ Here are five options to creatively and effectively provide childcare or eldercare:

○ Get one or more sitters for all of the kids, and have them watch the kids upstairs. Or, even better, find two homes in close proximity to one another. This way parents can drop the kids off at one home with the sitters and head to the other home for your group gathering. Schedule your group to begin fifteen minutes after drop-off.

○ Ask the high school group at church for volunteers to serve every week or every other week.

○ Ask your whole group to pitch in to pay for child or eldercare, even if they don't have kids or elderly parents themselves. Ask everyone to invest in everyone being there.

○ Structure monthly rotations for group gatherings such as:

◇ Week 1: Women only (where husbands/dads are with the kids/elderly parents)

◇ Week 2: Men only (where wives/moms are with the kids/elderly parents)

◇ Week 3: Adult members only (pay for childcare and/or eldercare)

◇ Week 4: Family gatherings, including small group members, their kids, and elderly parents

○ Invite the church to contribute financially to childcare and eldercare, making an investment in the church body to grow spiritually across the lifespan.[8]

Educators know about the power of a structured syllabus at the beginning of the first class. Students pore over those pages, looking for details about what's due when, what's expected of them, and how they can be successful. Professors who fail to give their students the detailed structure they need frustrate their students and often get off to a rocky start. Likewise, group leaders who don't provide structure inadvertently pave the way for unclear expectations and insecure followers, which rarely produces the positive outcomes for which they hope. New group members have many needs when they join a new group. Apply the Sample Agenda for Your Group's First Meeting to model the directive leadership your members need from you and lead an incredible first meeting.

TOOLS OF THE TRADE

SAMPLE AGENDA FOR YOUR GROUP'S FIRST MEETING

☐ Welcome the group.

☐ Clarify the purpose of the group (connecting it to your group members' felt needs).

☐ Get to know each other.

    ○ Complete introductions.

    ○ Do an introduction or icebreaker activity (see some of our favorites at thrivinggroups.com).

☐ Return to purpose. Ask people to comment on why they are there and what they wish to glean from the group, and revise/establish your group's purpose as necessary.

☐ Pray together, asking God to make that purpose happen.

☐ Try out whatever format your group will use (discuss sermon, do introduction to Bible study, etc.).

☐ Explain the initial structure for your group's next meeting— when, where, how to prepare for it, how long sessions will run, etc. (think of this as a syllabus for your group).

CAPTURE WHAT YOUR GROUP WILL DO AND HOW IN A GROUP COVENANT.

A group covenant includes an explanation of your group's purpose and what activities it will engage toward that purpose. It also outlines expectations for members. A group covenant is a great way to capture your group's key structures and ask members for their commitment to the group. Address when and how the group will meet and how members are expected to behave in group meetings as well as between them, and set expectations for treating one another with kindness, thoughtfulness, and care. Doing so will help you create an environment where people know what to expect from others and from themselves. Our study indicated that groups that not only established ground rules for how members were supposed to interact with each other, but then used those ground rules to hold members who violated them accountable, contributed more to members' spiritual growth. (Check out Appendix A at the back of the book, as well as the website, to find some sample group covenants.)

However, don't just have members sign the covenant and forget about it. This makes it a meaningless and futile exercise. Instead, revisit the covenant regularly, ask your group to comment on how well the group is living up to the covenant, and hold members accountable when they don't live up to the standards outlined in it.

TOOLS OF THE TRADE

SAMPLE AGENDA FOR YOUR GROUP'S SECOND MEETING

☐ Review your group's purpose.

☐ Continue to get to know each other: do something that helps people get to know each other a bit more (and become comfortable sharing).

☐ Set group expectations and ground rules that will help your group be effective. To develop a list of Dos and Don'ts, ask:

  ○ What do you love about groups?

  ○ What do you hate about groups?

☐ Sign a group covenant that captures the group's purpose and how it will work together (consider consulting with your ministry leader for a sample covenant).

☐ Begin pursuing your freshly articulated purpose.

DURING AND AFTER YOUR FIRST MEETINGS, CELEBRATE WILDLY!

As you're deploying that plan and walking through your first meeting or two, praise members who put themselves out there and demonstrate behaviors that you'd like others to engage in.

People are rarely more self-conscious than when they enter

groups for the first time. *Will they like me? Will I fit in here? How do I not make a fool of myself?* These are the questions people are asking. Maybe you, as the leader, are asking those questions, too. So answer them.

If someone pulls out a pack of gum and offers a piece to every member, celebrate them. "Wow, Bonnie, you are so thoughtful! I can't wait to be in this group with you this term." When Brian offers to close the evening in prayer, let the whole group know how grateful you are that he's willing to step out and participate, even at a first meeting. Not only will you encourage the person who contributed, but you will also indirectly communicate to other group members the kinds of actions that you desire.

The evidence that you've done this well won't look the way you expect. If you're successful in helping people walk through Stage One, your group will start to express differing and sometimes antagonistic opinions. Your group will feel like it is turning on you as its leader and engaging conflict with you and each other. And it'll be perfect—because that's exactly what needs to happen for your group to mature.

GUEST COMMENTARY

REACHING THE FRINGES

Chris Surratt

Small group connection events within the church have proven to be the best strategy for getting church members into a small group, but just pulling committed church people into our group should not be our only strategy. In fact, the small group invite is not even the best place to start if we want to truly engage those on the fringes of our churches and neighborhoods.

If we are following Jesus' Great Commission of making disciples, then it makes sense to also follow the pattern he modeled for us in forming community. We can see through Scripture that Jesus started with the people on the edges, drawing them deeper and deeper.

So where did Jesus start? He didn't look to gather a huge crowd or even a small group of people, but began in the community where he found himself. We can see this pattern starting with Jesus as a boy in the temple:

> After three days they found him in the temple, sitting among the teachers, listening to them and asking them questions. (Luke 2:46)

Jesus intentionally spent time with people and asked questions. He wanted to understand them before moving on to what was next. Our first "group" should be the community we find ourselves in: our neighborhoods, our coffee shops, our office, or anywhere we interact with people to ask questions and understand their stories and experiences. This is our first mission field. Look for those natural interactions that can lead to relationships.

Here are a few ideas to create those opportunities with your community:

1. **Throw a block party.** Everyone needs an excuse to get out and meet the neighbors, so you will be the star for providing one.
2. **Participate in Halloween.** Not everyone feels the same way about how to approach this holiday, but I don't know another occasion where most of my neighbors will not only be out of their houses at the same time but also spending a few minutes at mine.
3. **Host a movie on your lawn for the families in the neighborhood.** You can now affordably rent very large outdoor blow-up screens for your backyard. Put out a few flyers around the neighborhood and fire up the latest family-friendly blockbuster.

4. **Participate in neighborhood-sponsored events.** Some communities put on an Easter egg hunt or a quarterly "spruce up the 'hood" day.

5. **Be the nicest house on the block.** Everyone in the neighborhood knows the houses to avoid approaching. They all know to avoid the people who never acknowledge you when they're walking their dog. Be the complete opposite, and your neighbors will want to get to know you. Offer to loan out your grill for the neighborhood cookout. Mow the neighbor's lawn occasionally, just because you want to help.

Once you've established those relationships, you'll have opportunities to invite people to your small group. This is not a step that should be rushed. If the idea of being in a small group is completely foreign to someone, it will take a little bit of time and convincing before they are sitting in your living room. Don't give up!

Chris Surratt is discipleship and small groups specialist for LifeWay Christian Resources and the author of several books, including *Leading Small Groups: How to Gather, Launch, Lead, and Multiply Your Small Group.* Connect with Chris at ChrisSurratt.com.

KEY TAKEAWAYS: HOW TO SHIFT FROM *DISENGAGED TO DEDICATED* IN DIFFERENT GROUP SEASONS

WHEN LAUNCHING A NEW GROUP
1. Tell members what is expected of them.
2. Tap into people's felt needs when recruiting and inviting people into your group.
3. Personally invite the people you've identified to join the group.
4. Pray and plan your first gathering.
5. Address logistics challenges that might prevent full participation.
6. Follow through and do what you say you will do.
7. Make it easy for group members to contribute positively.

WHEN MAINTAINING A GROUP'S MOMENTUM AND EFFECTIVENESS
1. Immediately address members who don't show up. Let them know that you notice and care.
2. Consider how the members' needs change as the group proceeds.
3. Refresh your group covenant regularly (each session or 2–3 times/year).
4. Evaluate your current structure. To freshen group engagement, consider changing meeting time, venue, and activities.
5. Identify your core members and ask them to help grow your group.
6. Celebrate your group's good practices.
WHEN YOUR GROUP IS STRUGGLING
1. Identify and resolve problems with meeting time, location, and practices.
2. Ask the hard question: What value is lacking for you in being part of this group?
3. Revisit your group covenant, and refresh it as necessary.
4. Review past seasons when your group was fully devoted. What engaged your members?
5. Consult your coach or ministry team/staff member for support and suggestions.
6. Examine your core members' felt needs. Is it time to add more members?

REFLECTION AND DISCUSSION QUESTIONS

1. **Remember:** What caught your attention in this chapter about gathering and starting your group?

2. **Understand:** What do you now understand about the leader's role in starting successfully?

3. **Apply:** With regard to size, location, how you spend your time together, and other logistics, what can you put into practice immediately?

4. **Analyze:** How might a small adjustment in size, location, or how you spend your time together affect group life?

5. **Evaluate:** In humility, how has your inattention to developing key group structures or starting your group well hindered individual and group growth?

6. **Create:** For the next group or season, what plans would you make to provide good leadership from the very start?

CHAPTER 6

MINE TO OURS

Cultivate Commitment through Shared Ownership

*Responsibility equals accountability equals ownership.
And a sense of ownership is the most powerful
weapon a team or organization can have.*

—PAT SUMMITT

As they did most Friday evenings, the group had finished dinner and was wrapping up its discussion of the weekend sermon. Aaron, whose wife had become involved with another man and left their home months prior, intending to file for divorce, had faithfully attended the couples' group throughout the upheaval in his marriage. There was a break in the conversation, and he said, "I wanted to ask you guys something. I've reconnected with a girl I went to high school with. We've started talking, and I'd like her to come to our group sometime so you guys can meet."

Almost immediately, Miguel blurted out: "Wait, aren't you married? Did something change that I'm not aware of?"

Awkward silence ensued, and group members exchanged quick glances. Whoa! Aaron had just been really vulnerable by bringing up something close and personal. That was awesome. But Miguel got right up in his face and confronted him.

It was quite a moment.

John, the appointed group leader, felt this enormous pressure overwhelm him. He thought, *What do I say? How do I release the tension? Will Aaron ever come back?*

He fumbled, saying something along the lines of, "What Miguel is trying to say, I think, is . . ." and tried to soften Miguel's words. Others chimed in to explain that until Aaron was no longer married, he had no business hanging out with another woman. The conversation ended, the meeting concluded, and Aaron left. In the kitchen afterward, several ladies expressed concern that Miguel and John had been too harsh with Aaron and wondered if he'd ever come back.

The next day John called Aaron to check in. Almost immediately Aaron told him, "John, I broke it off with her. That was exactly what I needed to hear. I can't thank all of you enough for being willing to be honest with me."[1]

This chapter is all about how you can help cultivate the kind of group where conversations like that happen—where people are committed so much to God's work in them and to each other that they are willing to be vulnerable, to engage challenging conversations, to hear others, and to maintain relationships even in the midst of discomfort. In this kind of small group community, group members share their stories, actively listen to others' stories, spend time with one another outside of small group gatherings, and look forward to meaningfully contributing to their small group.

CATALYTIC LEADERS *CULTIVATE SHARED OWNERSHIP*

Catalytic Leaders...

Articulate Purpose.

Set the Stage.

Cultivate Shared Ownership.

Stimulate Meaningful Discussions.

Embrace Difficult Conversations.

In this chapter, we'll discuss how you, as a catalytic leader, can model and inspire commitment and spur ownership among your group members both during and between group meetings. As you do, you'll cultivate shared ownership of the group.

LEADERSHIP AND THE BODY OF CHRIST

In the story above, we focused on how John, the leader, reacted to the situation. This may have caused you to miss something important: ultimately, God used Miguel—Aaron's fellow group member—to speak truth into Aaron's situation. It was Miguel who played a significant role in preserving Aaron's family. That's what happens on a regular basis in thriving small groups.

But as we discussed in chapter 2, it is easy for leaders and members alike to believe that it's all (or mostly) about leaders and what they do, while underemphasizing the powerful role that members play. This often manifests in at least one of the following two ways. First, leaders can take on too much, which results in unnecessary stress and strain. Without intervention, these leaders experience burnout. Second, when leaders believe it's mostly about them, they don't readily see what their group members can contribute, let alone invite them to do so. This can result in a passive, consumeristic fellowship in which members arrive at meetings expecting to receive something without contributing anything. Then, when they don't get what they want, they stop coming.

The role of every member is also vitally important to the group.

Don't get us wrong: your role is important. But the role of every member is also vitally important to the group. This is reflected in Paul's message to the believers in Corinth many years ago. Take a moment to read through this passage with your small group in mind.

> For just as the body is one and has many members, and all the members of the body, though many, are one body, so it is with

Christ. For in one Spirit we were all baptized into one body—Jews or Greeks, slaves or free—and all were made to drink of one Spirit.

For the body does not consist of one member but of many. If the foot should say, "Because I am not a hand, I do not belong to the body," that would not make it any less a part of the body. And if the ear should say, "Because I am not an eye, I do not belong to the body," that would not make it any less a part of the body. If the whole body were an eye, where would be the sense of hearing? If the whole body were an ear, where would be the sense of smell? But as it is, God arranged the members in the body, each one of them, as he chose. If all were a single member, where would the body be? As it is, there are many parts, yet one body.

The eye cannot say to the hand, "I have no need of you," nor again the head to the feet, "I have no need of you." On the contrary, the parts of the body that seem to be weaker are indispensable, and on those parts of the body that we think less honorable we bestow the greater honor, and our unpresentable parts are treated with greater modesty, which our more presentable parts do not require. But God has so composed the body, giving greater honor to the part that lacked it, that there may be no division in the body, but that the members may have the same care for one another. If one member suffers, all suffer together; if one member is honored, all rejoice together.

Now you are the body of Christ and individually members of it. (1 Cor. 12:12–27)

Leaders of the most effective groups recognize their humble responsibilities while also recognizing everyone else's unique contributions. On a practical level, the leader's job is to structure the group for success, to facilitate group interactions that build upon and bring together every member's contributions, and to help the group cooperatively accomplish its purpose and goals. That leaves a lot of room for others to contribute.

THE QUESTION OF OWNERSHIP: MINE OR OURS

As we shared in the previous chapter, if you're leading your group well through the first stage of group development, your members are learning what behavior is acceptable in the group, and they're leaning on you for direction. As groups work through that initial stage, group members will begin to share their own ideas and challenge the leader's authority. That's a really good thing. Group development research shows that as the group does this, they're beginning to utilize a structure for engaging together and building trusting relationships.

What does this mean for your leadership?

Remember, you've just gone through the stage of group formation where everyone is looking to and leaning on you. That can be daunting and dazzling all at once. You'll be tempted to continue your directive leadership, keeping members dependently leaning on and looking to you. After all, things are moving forward, right?

Here's the problem: leader-only ownership is a ticking time bomb for burnout. You might have another six months. If you've got really high stamina, if you're really skilled in organizing and prioritizing, if you're particularly self-aware, and if your group members are really cooperative, you might last four years or so. But the ending will be the same.

About three months into his first role as a small groups pastor, Jason facilitated a training on leader self-care. At the end of that training, two of his leaders indicated they were quitting. Within a week, that number had jumped to four. All of them had been leading for about two years. Each of them had privately expressed similar sentiments: they loved their groups but were too tired to continue.

Through the conversations, the leaders began to describe all that they did for their group: scheduling food, recording and sending out prayer requests, securing childcare, following up with every single person outside of group time, organizing and taking meals to group members, talking with the church about service opportunities, and more. The combined responsibilities became overwhelming, and the leaders were worn out, tired, disappointed in themselves, and left with the conclusion that it was time to step down. In their own way, they all implicitly felt similarly: "I can't carry the weight for my group anymore. Maybe I'm not cut out for this. My group deserves better."

For your group to be the best group it can be, you need to ask yourself who owns the group: "Is this 'my group' or 'our group'?"

TWO-MINUTE TIP

Send a quick text or email to a trusted member of the small group you lead inviting them to coffee to talk about your leadership tendencies:

- Do you share logistical responsibilities with members?
- Do you feel comfortable asking for and receiving help from the group?
- Do members increasingly take on tasks and responsibilities based on their passions and giftings?
- Are members engaged in serving others inside and outside the group?

Inviting a group member into discussion about these questions can help you determine the group's current state of ownership.

Great leaders work themselves out of playing too big a role by moving group members from consuming to contributing. In particular, one of your biggest roles is to incrementally and strategically encourage every member to become a dynamic part of the group. Doing so takes creativity and patience, but breathes life and sets up your group for ongoing success and spiritual growth.

As we've already discussed, when a group first starts out, the members look to the leader for everything. But when group members start following, great leaders know it's time to start giving away their leadership. Great leaders understand that when they say "no," others will be invited to say "yes."

Great leaders take on the responsibility but keep the end goal in mind: shared ownership. Thus starts the dance we described in chapter 3, where you invite members to take a step forward. As they step forward, you step back and encourage them to take another step forward. In return, you step back even more. Not too quickly, but not too slowly.

TRANSFORM CONSUMERS INTO CONTRIBUTORS

Based on our study, we've identified three specific actions you can take to encourage your members to commit and engage rather than just showing up and consuming.

SHARE STORIES

One of the ways you can elicit more ownership is to encourage group members to share their stories and share more of themselves as your group develops. Our study found that groups who invite their members to share their stories, and take time to *learn* each other's stories have a greater effect on members' spiritual health. Beth, a small group leader in Pennsylvania, found that sharing stories fostered greater group ownership in her group: "Almost immediately, our group had conversations that went far beyond the surface level because we shared our stories right at the beginning of our group." When you and your group are sharing your stories, you're doing more than answering questions that seek specific, correct answers. You're sharing life.

As a leader, you must remember that it takes courage for your group members to be vulnerable with their life stories. You can help your group members gain courage by not only creating space for them to share, but by sharing your own story. By doing so, you're modeling what you want your group to be about and inviting other group members to participate. Priest and author Henri Nouwen reminds us that we are created to be known and that sharing our stories connects us to one another at the deepest parts of ourselves. We are called to lead not as "'professionals' who know their 'client' problems and take care of them, but vulnerable brothers and sisters who know and are known, who care and are cared for, who forgive and are forgiven, who love and are being loved. Somehow we have come to believe that good leadership requires a safe distance from those we are called to lead."[2]

Being known starts with you.

Leaders who do *not* share their own stories may inhibit group growth. In fact, our research revealed that when leaders limit their own responses or withhold their own participation, groups contribute *significantly less* to members' spiritual growth.

Early on in the life of his small group, Sam, a small group leader on the West Coast, would ask for volunteers to share parts of their testimony. Someone would reluctantly oblige. Their responses were never what Sam hoped. Sometimes they were long-winded, sometimes they were seemingly irrelevant, and sometimes they were filled with hurt without hope. Like many leaders, Sam wanted his group members to share first. He wanted to encourage his group members to participate and model humility as a leader—both noble goals. But he failed to recognize that his group was still in that first stage of group development where members grow when leaders lead, helping discussions stay on topic and intervening when dominating members begin to take over. Especially in this early stage, group members *want* and need their leaders to share their own stories, opinions, and expertise, and facilitate others sharing well. In fact, the group's contribution to spiritual growth decreases when leaders don't also personally contribute to conversations and discussions.

> Be open about your doubts, your struggles, and your victories. In doing so, you will point your group members to Jesus.

When you model vulnerability by sharing your stories, members who are still getting to know you and other group members are more willing to trust you and your leadership. While group members don't want their leaders to be complete disasters, they *do* want them to be real people with legitimate struggles who are fighting the good fight with great hope. So be open about your doubts, your struggles, and your victories. In doing so, you will point your group members to Jesus.

TWO-MINUTE TIP

There are multiple ways to share your story; choose one that is comfortable for you. Here is one method that is quick and to the point. Based upon Paul's teaching in Colossians 1:21–23, take a couple of minutes and complete each of the following statements:

I once was . . .
Jesus has . . .
I am now . . .

You can add more details as you practice this, but consider sharing this version in your next group gathering and encouraging your members to do the same.

INVEST IN THE OTHER 165.75 HOURS

In chapter 5, we explained that the most effective groups in our study met for more than two hours and fifteen minutes. But what should happen during the other 165.75 hours of the week? How much effort should you put into connecting and communicating during that time?

Your group's purpose should drive the answer to this question, at least partially. How your group interacts (or doesn't) outside of established gathering times can influence how much progress you make toward your group's purpose. If your group is centered on gathering in public places to pray for and with non-believers, then your group will meet more often outside of the designated weekly gathering. If your group has a focus on biblical hospitality, members might pair up to live out hospitality together at the park, a shared workplace, or a coffee shop.

Whatever your group's purpose, don't underestimate the importance of ongoing communication with group members. Our study found that the more leaders communicated with their members (as reported by members, not leaders themselves), the more the group contributed to its members' spiritual growth. In fact, a leader's frequency of communication is an excellent predictor of the group's value in encouraging spiritual growth.

One of the most important things you can do as a leader for your group is to contact them. Call them, email them, text them, or send a note via carrier pigeon or smoke signal. Find a way that works for you and your group members, then use it. Regularly.

Your engagement as a leader sets the tone for group member interaction. And it's your opportunity as a leader to model that behavior for others to follow. As the chart below indicates, members of the most effective groups reported that their leader communicated with them more than once a week, but not quite every day. While most leaders reported sending an email once a week, the frequency of communication includes group emails and group text messages, but also one-to-one communication. In practice, this might mean one or two group emails (perhaps a prayer recap email and a reminder about the gathering next week) and an individual one-to-one phone call, text message, or email. This regularity of communication (in the eyes of your members) is related to the group's contribution to individuals'

HOW OFTEN LEADERS COMMUNICATE WITH
MEMBERS BETWEEN MEETINGS

Great group leaders	Several times per week
Average group leaders	Once a week
Below-average group leaders	Once or twice per month

spiritual health. What starts as "best practice" and perfunctory often turns into genuine friendship and authentic concern for others.

So what are the best ways to connect with group members?

There isn't one best way, no one silver bullet. We found that group members and leaders rarely use phone calls or the church's website or app to communicate with others. Instead, they mostly utilize texts and emails, in that order.

When we asked pastors and ministry leaders how their group leaders effectively communicate with group members, they listed methods including text, email, the Group Me app, church database tools, closed Facebook groups, Snapchat, WhatsApp, and, of course, in-person interactions. Good options abound.

This pastor's response seemed to summarize our findings: "We tried to find a solution that would work for all small groups, but each group is unique in its needs. Instead, coaches are trained to ask their leaders how they communicate. The goal is for all groups to find a tool that aligns with the goals of the group."

Sara, a group leader from Illinois who believes following up with group members is critical, emphasized that whatever frequency of communication or method you use, "It has to be doable so that you actually do it."

Find what works for you. Use reminders on your phone, in your planner, and on your computer. Consider scheduling a text, email, or phone call with one of your members every morning at 10 a.m.

Here's the big picture: when you invest time in the other 165.75 hours, members will feel seen and known. And when they walk through the door for your weekly group gathering feeling seen and known, they'll do more than just show up. They'll engage with and invest in the group because you've engaged with and invested in them.

In fact, in the most effective groups in our study—groups wherein individuals are growing spiritually as a result of the group—70 percent of members connect with at least one other member outside the regularly scheduled group gathering at least once a month, and 65 percent of groups interacted at least twice a month outside the regularly scheduled group gatherings. Those are staggering numbers!

Additionally, as we shared earlier, the more the leader is committed to the group, the more the group contributes to its members' spiritual growth. This appeared in the leaders' self-reports of their own levels of commitment to the group, but the effect was even stronger when group members reported their leaders' commitment to the group. And when leaders communicated frequently with their group members, as often as "almost every day," group members perceived the leader was highly committed to the group. Send a text today!

TWO-MINUTE TIP

Send a quick text, draft a group email, or make calls to your group members. Ask them to tell you their preferred method of communication, and how they'd like to connect with other group members in between gatherings. Then, once you hear from them, set up the mechanism (an email distribution list, a group text, or whatever) so you can take action. Then, use your new tool so they know you heard them.

IDENTIFY AND DELEGATE LEADERSHIP OPPORTUNITIES

When group members share their stories, connect during the week between group gatherings, and begin to invest in the group, they'll start to make bids for ownership. This might look like volunteering to fill in gaps you didn't see (like Miguel did in John's story), making suggestions for how your group should spend its time, or challenging your plan or approach. And we'll say it again—this is a good thing!

Delegation is an art that expands the boundaries and opportunities for group member ownership. When delegating, consider the following two principles.

First, delegate *authority* rather than tasks. If you value shared ownership and then expect bids of ownership, be prepared to give away your ownership for the sake of the group. To the extent that you can, give away ownership of whole tasks rather than breaking them up. Ask someone to take on the responsibility of leading your prayer time or sending out a recap of key prayer requests. Invite a couple of members to organize your group's food plan or put together your next service project.

By giving away whole chunks of group life, you show confidence in your members' abilities and spur shared ownership more quickly. If, by contrast, you ask a member to help you by handling only part of a larger task, you haven't really given it away—you've just recruited an assistant. Delegating authority produces trust and accountability.

Remember, the goal is to dance yourself out of a role. In order to do this, you have to give it away, strategically and incrementally, until every member has an equal level of ownership with you.

Second, delegate anything and everything group members can do themselves. Parents tend to do a lot for their children. When they see a need, they meet it—or take steps to eliminate a problem before it even surfaces. This works when children are toddlers, but eventually, they need and want to make decisions on their own. This same mentality creeps into group life and creates a culture of dependence. Delegation, on the other hand, creates a culture of contribution.

What are a few things you can prepare in advance to give away? Consider areas such as hospitality, location of the gathering, serving opportunities, and inviting new members to the group. These are great areas where group members can take the lead. In the following paragraphs, we'll offer some suggestions for how to facilitate these handoffs.

Hospitality

Hospitality is more than the provision of food and drinks. However, food and drink tend to be a common and sometimes taxing part of any group, and the task of organizing refreshments is something that leaders can readily give away.

Imagine one of your group members approaches you and asks, "Do you think we could do something besides pizza next week?"

Before you get your feathers ruffled and defend the decision you've been making, recognize this as a bid for shared ownership. That's a win, so celebrate it! Then use it as an opportunity to delegate.

Say, "Sure! And thanks, Angela, for noticing. What ideas do you have for dinner next week?"

Invite group members into the process of planning for next week's meal. And if that goes well, at the end of next week's meeting, invite the group to facilitate meal planning yet again. When you get the sense that someone is ready to take leadership of food and drinks, hand it off!

TOOLS OF THE TRADE

MANAGING GROUP MEALS

Eating together? Here are a few meal planning strategies:

☐ Invite a group member to own and be responsible for planning and communicating weekly meal plans.

☐ Ask one member to ask everyone to bring something every time.

☐ Have one person provide the main dish and each of your other four group members bring a salad, a side dish, drinks, and a dessert, respectively. (See thrivinggroups.com for some ready-to-use meal plans.)

☐ Ask for volunteers to provide an entire meal or dessert for the entire group once per session.

Venue, Starting Time, and Other Logistics

Maybe you've heard off-handed comments about how far away your gathering place is from where your group members live. Or you start to notice that most members are arriving twenty minutes after the established start time. Or a member confronts you about how hard it is to get to work early the next morning because the group went until 10 p.m.

It's not an attack. Or a threat. It's a bid for group ownership.

So give away your ownership and honor their bid for it. Say something like:

"I can see that the home where we're meeting is far from a lot of you. Can you think creatively about a place further south of town and bring a couple options for discussion next week?"

"I've noticed that many of you are arriving closer to 7 p.m. than 6:30 p.m. Should we be starting group at 7 p.m. instead, or can we provide dinner so you can come straight from work and honor that 6:30 start time?"

"I hear that concern about ending late. What time do you think we should plan to finish our group discussions so that you continue to reap the benefits of the group while also being rested for the next day?"

As group members offer feedback about group goals, roles, and structures, shared ownership will emerge. Over time, those bids for group ownership will lead to productive conversations, which in turn develops trust. Let this feedback happen. Embrace it! Because when you see that happening, even if it makes you feel uncomfortable and like you're no longer in control, you'll see your group members becoming more deeply invested and growing together.

Engaging Service Opportunities

Give away the coordination of service projects, meal trains, baby showers, or whatever else your group takes on. For example, a member of Jason's current small group coordinates partnerships with a local nonprofit that connects people to serve and support the foster care community. This group member directs the entire group to serving opportunities.

Facilitating Elements of Group Gatherings

One of the most potent lies about the leadership of small groups is the expectation that the leader should do everything for the group. This lie is further exacerbated by the culture of consumption prevalent in much of North American culture. It rears its ugly head in group life when the leader or group members expect the leader to do and be everything for them. The more you delegate, the more you directly combat this culture and help create a culture of contribution.

We are not suggesting wholesale surrender of your leadership; rather, we're suggesting you recruit a team of leaders and train them to lead. Teams of leaders are almost always better than single leaders, but only if those teams share authority and responsibility for providing leadership. Thus, small group leaders should seek to work themselves out of the *sole* leadership role, and toward recruiting and raising up new leaders, and leading new, multiplied groups. Make that your goal, too! (We'll discuss this leadership development function in chapter 10.)

GETTING CLOSER TO THE PROMISED LAND

Group ownership propels group growth and leadership sustainability. As group members realize how they can actively contribute, the group grows to more effectively accomplish its purpose. Sharing stories, listening well, investing outside of official group gatherings, and helping members contribute in significant ways to the group all help members experience and feel ownership at a deeper level. Great leaders dance their way out of the primary leadership role by encouraging members to contribute and supporting them in their contributions.

As your leadership moves from *mine* to *ours*, you will have built an incredible climate of shared ownership. Now, you can turn your attention to crafting powerful group gatherings. But that doesn't come naturally for anyone. Learning how to craft and ask good questions and facilitate transformational conversations will propel your group forward and deepen the opportunity for tangible growth. That's your next shift.

GUEST COMMENTARY

How My 12-Step Group Changed the Way I Lead Small Groups

Vivian Mabuni

I sat on my hands, hoping it would still my beating heart. Over a couple of decades serving in vocational Christian ministry, I had led, organized, and facilitated small groups on college campuses and in churches. This time, however, I came as a brand-new attendee, and all I could think was, "I'm living that scene with the sharks in recovery in *Finding Nemo*."

We went around the circle and introduced ourselves by our first names. "Hi. I'm Vivian. And I think I'm codependent. Today I feel . . ." One after another, we shared our stories and learned about listening without fixing, not seeking to over-spiritualize, not one-upping what someone shared, and respecting a set time in order to make sure the maximum number of people had the opportunity to contribute. Most importantly, we provided safety in committing to total confidentiality. Week after week, I would leave my first experience with a 12-step group for Co-dependents Anonymous thinking, "This is how the church and God's people were meant to connect. This picture of safety, honesty, vulnerability, and truth is what is often missing in small groups."

Looking back, my years invested in the 12-step group challenged and shaped how I would lead small groups in the future. Over and over, the most successful groups I've led and in which I've participated have all had the qualities of safety, honesty, confidentiality, truth, and vulnerability. When those elements are present, I find the group members begin to move towards true ownership.

I've noticed that at least two distinct shifts take place when small group members move toward shared ownership. The first is a change in language from referring to belonging to or attending "*your*" Bible study to embracing the group and describing it as "*our*" small group. The shift of shared ownership changes the person's tone and even the priority level of the group.

The second shift is when group members begin sharing prayer requests that move beyond the health concerns of their neighbors. When people request prayer that involves personal hardship, I know the group is moving toward shared ownership. The groups I've led that experienced high attendance and commitment are those in which members communicated with honesty about their real-life struggles. An environment of trust is built when the leader not only sets expectations of confidentiality, but also leads out in sharing real issues and authentically discloses current life challenges.

I've served in vocational Christian ministry for thirty years and led small groups for even longer. The best groups have been those in which there was shared ownership. The greatest growth has occurred in groups where members' lives intersected deeply through the act of carrying one another's burdens in an environment of safety and commitment to holding confidence. The health and maturing God intends for his people cannot be attained in isolation. Intimacy with God is activated and achieved as we live out the truths found in the Word of God in community with others.

Vivian Mabuni has served 30 years on staff with Cru, is the author of *Warrior in Pink* and *Open Hands, Willing Heart*, and is the host of the podcast *Someday Is Here*. Learn more at VivianMabuni.com or connect with her @vivmabuni.

KEY TAKEAWAYS: HOW TO SHIFT FROM *MINE TO OURS* IN DIFFERENT GROUP SEASONS

WHEN LAUNCHING A NEW GROUP
1. Take delegating slowly. Too much too quickly will stress out members.
2. As soon as members offer feedback and suggestions, listen to their input and make adjustments.
3. Invite people to help with meal planning, childcare, managing logistics, and planning service/ministry.
4. Know and share your own story with your group.

WHEN MAINTAINING GROUP'S MOMENTUM AND EFFECTIVENESS
1. Develop a plan to hear every group member's story. Maybe it's one story a week.
2. Invite members to take on leadership roles.
3. Take a different group member out for coffee or lunch every other week to hear more about his or her life.
4. Connect group members with one another outside of group gatherings.

WHEN YOUR GROUP IS STRUGGLING
1. Plan or facilitate gatherings and connection points in the other 165.75 hours.
2. Ask the hard question: What value is lacking for you in being part of this group?
3. Commit to touching base with each member every other week.
4. Strategically ask group members to connect with each other.
5. Consider meeting in a new location and/or on a new day/time.

REFLECTION AND DISCUSSION QUESTIONS

1. **Remember:** What caught your attention in this chapter about cultivating shared ownership?
2. **Understand:** What does it mean for a leader to move group members from *consuming* to *contributing*?
3. **Apply:** In what area of group life can you give away ownership immediately?
4. **Analyze:** If you were out of the country for a month, what do you think might happen with your group gatherings?
5. **Evaluate:** How would you evaluate your willingness to give away your leadership? What keeps you from being more willing?
6. **Create:** Imagine that you are not able to lead your group for four weeks in the near future. What plans for shared leadership do you need to implement in order to cultivate continued individual and group growth?

TRIVIAL TO TRANSFORMATIVE

Stimulate Meaningful Discussions

*Good teaching is more a giving of right
questions than a giving of right answers.*

—JOSEF ALBERS

The dreaded silence.

Every leader knows what we're talking about. You've opened your group time with prayer, shared a delicious meal and casual conversation, watched a video teaching and read through Scripture, and now you've jumped into discussion questions. Things were going fine until you asked that last question. Silence. It seems to go on forever—at least until you grow uncomfortable enough to rephrase the question or move on to the next topic.

Or maybe silence has never been an issue for your group. Maybe the issue is *that* member—the one who dominates the conversation and is the first to contribute to group discussions. Every. Single. Time.

She is the loudest, and not just in volume. She always has a response. She might even be the wisest and most biblically literate group member you have. But while most of the time she has something valuable to contribute, you find yourself secretly relieved when she can't make it to your small group gathering because other members only contribute in her absence.

Been there? We all have.

Both of these are common problems for small group leaders. And here's part of the reason why: in our study, small groups pastors reported that the top three qualities they look for in identifying and recruiting leaders are personal integrity, teachability, and personal spiritual maturity. And that's beautiful—there is nothing inherently wrong with those qualities. But when we asked small group leaders what they needed help with, most of them wanted to learn how to encourage good dialogue.

See the knowledge gap? Pastors recruit leaders based on their personal integrity, teachability, and personal spiritual maturity, not their ability to facilitate fruitful group discussions.

It might be tempting to conclude that pastors should start recruiting leaders based on their teaching abilities or their skill in facilitating discussions, but that's not the right solution. Leaders can be *taught* how to facilitate good discussions, but we can't teach integrity, teachability, or spiritual maturity (at least not easily!).

CATALYTIC LEADERS *STIMULATE MEANINGFUL DISCUSSIONS*

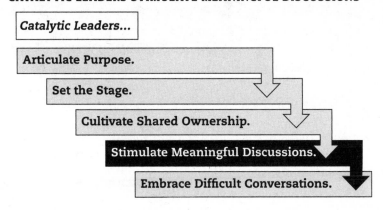

In this chapter, we're going to step into that gap and teach you the best practices of facilitation.

Our study suggests that high-quality group discussions have a positive effect on members' spiritual health. In the most effective groups, members contributed equally to discussion and talked among themselves, rather than speaking solely to the leader. Our findings align with recent research, which found that members of successful teams talk and listen in roughly equal measure, and members face one another and connect directly with one another, not just with the team leader.[1]

The best group discussions are generally those in which group members speak to one another. This is opposed to discussions in which a leader asks a question, one member responds, and then the leader asks another question, which resembles a tennis coach serving tennis balls to one player at a time. Remember, the goal is for all members to feel *invited* to participate in the discussion. Thus, great leaders volley with their group, rather than set up to serve with each comment and question.

FACILITATING A GROUP CONVERSATION*

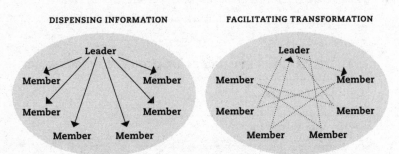

*Adapted from Gladen's Leading Small Groups with Purpose.[2]

Aside from contributing to greater spiritual health, discussion quality also has a significant effect on aging groups. Our research showed that groups tend to experience spiritual growth early on in their lifecycles and level out over time. This is likely the result of groups moving into more of a maintenance stage rather than a growth stage as members become more familiar with one another and settle into group norms. But when groups engage in high-quality discussions, they can almost entirely counteract the decay they would otherwise experience over time. Simply put, quality discussion creates continued spiritual growth.

So how can you improve the quality of discussions in your group? Let's start with best practices during meetings.

> When groups engage in high-quality discussions, they can almost entirely counteract the decay they would otherwise experience over time.

ASK BETTER QUESTIONS

Questions are powerful—sometimes more powerful than we acknowledge. Unaware of how to use questions well, leaders unnecessarily bring uncertainty into their group discussions.

Questions are like tools. Different kinds of tools do different things. You shouldn't use a hammer when you need a wrench, and you shouldn't use a highlighter when a pen is more appropriate. Understanding the uses of different types of questions will help you choose questions more deliberately and appropriately and see better outcomes.

Great leaders ask questions that facilitate group discussion rather than fish for a right answer. There are few things less engaging than being asked questions that have one "right" answer. When members recognize that there's only one answer to a question, they will be less likely to participate in the conversation. This is in part because people yield to one another, and no one wants to be the one person to correctly answer the question and squelch further discussion. Group members hold back lest they look like a know-it-all or answer incorrectly.

When you understand the power of questions and readily recognize the purpose of the group and the goals of group discussion, you will better utilize questions to achieve those ends. In the following paragraphs, we'll discuss types of questions both to use and to avoid in order to encourage discussion rather than squelch it.

AVOID FOUR COMMON QUESTION PITFALLS

Because small group leaders often ask questions on the spot, they may stumble into these four common question pitfalls without realizing it. We want to help you become aware of these types of questions so you can avoid asking them.

1. Bipolar Questions

Open and closed questions vary in the amount of information they solicit and the degree of control the question asker exerts over responses. Open questions give group members considerable freedom to determine what kind of information and how much to give, while closed questions are narrower in focus and restrict group members' freedom to determine the type and amount of information they share.

Bipolar questions assume that there are only two possible answers. While the most common answers these questions generate are "yes" or "no," they may also generate an "agree" or "disagree" response, or "approve" or "disapprove." Either way, the possible answers are on opposite poles. Here are a few examples of bipolar questions:

> *Did you like Sunday's sermon?*
> *Do you have any questions?*

Eliminate bipolar questions by beginning questions with words or phrases such as *what, why, how, explain,* and *tell us about.* Better questions than the ones above may be:

> *What did you appreciate most about Sunday's sermon?*
> *What questions do you have?*

2. "Tell Me Everything" Questions

"Tell me everything" questions are the opposite of bipolar questions. While bipolar questions restrict the possible answers too much, "tell me everything" questions are extremely open and offer no restrictions or guidelines for members to follow. Here are a few examples:

> *Can we please introduce ourselves? Let's go around the room.*
> *What challenges have you experienced in the past?*

Questions like these leave members uncertain what to include, what to exclude, and when to end.

What is a good balance in asking questions? Ask more open questions than closed questions, but don't make them too open. Rather than saying, "Let's go around and introduce ourselves," you might say:

> *Can we please go around and introduce ourselves?*
> *Please share how long you've been attending Oaks Church, what you*
> *hope our small group will be, and your favorite thing to do on a*
> *Saturday morning.*

This helps members know that they don't need to tell their life stories, and it provides some guardrails to help members stay on track.

3. Double-Barreled Inquisition Questions

The double-barreled inquisition question occurs when you ask two or more questions at the same time.

> *What did you learn from this passage, and how does it apply to*
> *your life?*
> *When have you experienced God's provision, and how did it change*
> *your outlook?*

Double-barreled inquisition questions often overwhelm members, producing decades of silence. Or members will only answer the part of the question that they remember, forcing you to repeat the other part at some point. Avoid this pitfall by only asking one question at a time.

4. The Leading Push Question

The fourth common pitfall is called the *leading push* question. Courtney vividly remembers being asked one of these questions at church just weeks after she and her husband got married:

> *Isn't married life amazing?*

As she tells the story to others, she usually points out that the response options are, "Yes," and "YES!" The *leading push* question occurs when you ask a question that suggests how your members should respond. While some pushes are intentional, others are unintentional, and your verbal and nonverbal communication can project feelings and attitudes that restrict members' freedom to respond. Other examples include:

> *You're going to the women's gathering Friday, right?*
> *You don't actually believe that, do you?*

The trouble with these questions is that members may simply go along with whatever answer you seem to want, especially when you, the leader, are the one asking the question. When your goal is to facilitate spiritual growth, phrase questions neutrally and listen carefully to the way you ask them. This will give your members freedom to respond in ways that encourage additional dialogue.

REALIZE YOUR QUESTIONS MATTER

As you develop questions for your discussions, remember this major principle: *What* you ask and *how* you ask will communicate what you know and how much you care.

> **What you ask and how you ask will communicate what you know and how much you care.**

Asking more open questions, while avoiding the bipolar trap and "tell me everything" questions, communicates that you invite a variety of answers, don't have any specific "right" answer in mind, while still giving group members guardrails for their responses. By asking one question at a time, you avoid double-barreled inquisitions, better directing members about how to engage; by avoiding leading push questions, you invite authenticity by encouraging freedom and openness.

When you better understand what kinds of responses particular questions can provoke, you'll choose better questions, which will produce more fruitful discussions. This, in turn, will incite spiritual growth in the members of your group.

TWO-MINUTE TIP

Take a few minutes to tune up the quality of your questions. Can you spot the better questions for a small group gathering? Cross out the questions that represent one of the pitfalls described above:

We're talking about friendship today. Tell us about the most important quality of one of your earliest childhood friends.	We're talking about friendship today. Tell us about one of your best friends.
You were challenged by Sunday's message like I was, right?	How were you encouraged by Sunday's message?
Can you think of a time when you experienced conflict in the church and what you learned from it?	When you think about a time when you've experienced conflict in the church, what did you learn about God, yourself, or others?
How many of you noticed the shift in tone from verse 24 to 25?	What did you notice about the shift in tone from verse 24 to 25?
How was your week?	After our discussion last week about prayer, please share one way in which you experienced the power of prayer this week.

STRATEGICALLY SEQUENCE YOUR QUESTIONS

Unfortunately, great group discussion isn't achieved just by avoiding common pitfall questions. *Question sequence* matters, too.

The order in which leaders ask questions can facilitate or inhibit learning and discussion. There's nothing worse than when a group leader starts out a discussion with a really heavy opening question, such as:

When in your life have you felt most distant from God?

This type of question can be challenging for group members no matter when you ask it, but can be particularly harmful at the very beginning of a group discussion, because it can require group members to go too deep, too quickly. A group discussion can also be challenging when it remains surface-level for a full two hours, with the leader only asking questions about what group members recall or remember about a particular text. A leader's ability to maneuver the ebbs and flows of discussion contributes to a fruitful learning process.

Catalytic leaders learn how to meet group members where they are and lead them through the learning and growing process. This can be achieved by using one or both of the following methods: Bloom's Taxonomy and/or the inverted funnel sequence.

Many educators are familiar with Bloom's Taxonomy of Learning, Teaching, and Assessing.[3] This framework describes the learning process and articulates educational goals, which generally move from simple to complex and concrete to abstract. Imagine that your small group has just engaged a video sermon or message about gospel-driven work. We'll use the six-phase taxonomy to show you how to lead group members through this learning process.

🖐 REMEMBER

Before group members can engage in discussion, they must recall and recognize what they're discussing. In the case of debriefing the above-mentioned video sermon or message about gospel-driven work, you might start by reviewing what was presented before moving on. Get everyone on the same page.

🦉 UNDERSTAND

You can't understand, summarize, or explain what you don't recall. If group members don't remember the content from the video, you can't expect them to understand it. That's like asking a five-year-old how he put together last year's Christmas present. He can't remember what gifts he received, let alone explain a particular process. Adults operate similarly—we must remember before we can understand.

⚙️ APPLY

In order to apply information, you need to first remember it and understand it. Only when one remembers and understands the video about how the gospel impacts work can one then embrace opportunities to apply the gospel to one's individual work life. By first knowing what God does in the creation story and understanding it, you can then apply work practices that reflect the Creator. Understanding gospel-driven work can then be applied toward considering and observing a six-day workweek and Sabbath rhythm.

🔍 ANALYZE

Analyzing means to differentiate, organize, and attribute. In a small group discussion, it may mean moving group members from applying a biblical theology of work to differentiating between Christian and non-Christian workplaces.

📋 EVALUATE

After analyzing, we can then grow more complex in our thinking through checking and critiquing. Through evaluation, we learn more about ourselves in relation to God, critiquing our work lives and relationships in light of the gospel.

💡 CREATE

The last category includes producing, generating, and planning. As a result of walking through this learning process, individual members or the group as a whole may be poised to generate new gospel-driven endeavors for cultural renewal in their workplaces.

When you, as a small group leader, understand the concepts above, you will be more readily able to engage your members in the learning process through discussion facilitation. You'll ask better questions to meet group members where they are and lead them deeper.

Practically, you can do this by crafting your question sequences with care. While there are many question sequences, we'll introduce you to one that may be helpful in guiding your discussion: the *inverted funnel sequence.*

THE INVERTED FUNNEL SEQUENCE

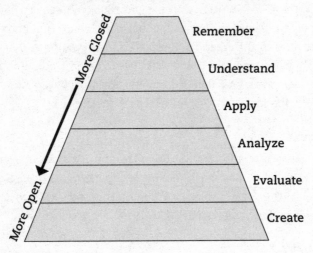

The inverted funnel sequence begins with closed questions and progresses to open questions. This is a great strategy if you find yourself needing to motivate your group members to respond or you sense some "warm-up" questions might help get the discussion going. The following reflects an inverted funnel sequence and Bloom's Taxonomy:

1. 🖐 **Remember:** In this passage of Scripture, who are the main characters?
2. 🖐🦉 **Remember/Understand:** What do we see them doing?

3. ✸ **Apply:** When we see Jesus in his proper place in the story, what can we take away?

4. ✸ **Apply:** What might you do this week in light of what we've learned?

5. 🔍 **Analyze:** After applying Jeremiah 29, what other biblical stories do you recall that also engage this doctrine of exile?

TWO-MINUTE TIP

At your next group meeting, ask a member or a co-leader to write down all the questions you ask during the group discussion. Then, on your own time, review all the questions you asked. Take note of which questions didn't work, and rewrite any questions that you identify as a common pitfall question. Then, see if you can identify the kinds of learning that each of your questions produced. Does your line of questioning follow the learning process similarly? What adjustments might you make for your next meeting?

One last nugget: our study revealed that the group contributed to members' spiritual health when leaders asked *relational questions*. Relational questions are those in which leaders asked members how they feel about each other, the group, and the discussion at hand. These types of questions could also be categorized as "Apply" questions. Going back to our discussion on sequencing, however, members must *remember* and *understand* before they get to these kinds of questions.

With this increased awareness of the power of questions and the choices you have in sequencing your questions, you can catalyze better group discussions. In fact, we found that group leaders who asked more open-ended questions were more likely to contribute to individuals' spiritual health. When you ask better questions, you're inviting members to engage and participate with each other, and you're strategically leading your group members through the learning process. Don't you agree? (Wait, was that just a leading push question?)

TWO-MINUTE TIP

As you grow in your mastery of questions, here are a few to keep in your back pocket:

- What caught your attention in the first paragraph of the passage?
- And what else?
- Tell us more.
- Can anyone speak into that?
- How have you seen this played out this week?
- What will you do in response to this teaching?
- What has become clearer to you since we last connected?

DESIGN INTERACTIONS WITH INTENTION

Almost as important as the questions you ask are the contexts in which you ask them. Earlier, we asked you to strategically consider the location of your group meetings. Maybe you're deciding between a small home and a more spacious coffee shop and are considering the variables that characterize each. Once you've reached your decision, it's time to consider your seating arrangement. But don't stop there. Seating arrangement is just one of the many dynamics that help design interaction.

PAY ATTENTION TO EYE CONTACT

Nonverbal communication research suggests that one-way leaders signal turn-taking is by making eye contact.[4] Your group isn't in kindergarten, so your group members shouldn't need to raise their hands to get your permission to speak. Instead, you can acknowledge a group member's desire to speak by making eye contact. The way your seats are arranged is going to influence which members you make eye contact with most. So as you think about that most talkative member, is it possible that you inadvertently encourage her to speak based on your position in the room?

It doesn't matter as much as you might think if everyone doesn't participate in the group equally. But members should feel invited into the conversation.

If you have a dominating, talkative member, you likely also have at least a few quiet members. You may sense that a quieter member has something to contribute, but after the talkative member's long, drawn-out contribution, everyone else is ready to move on. When your group members begin to feel like there's no time for them to share, they're less likely to engage in and benefit from the group.

You can leverage eye contact to influence turn-taking and facilitate better discussions. Sit next to a talkative member rather than across from them (see the figure below). This makes it more difficult for dominating members to make eye contact with you and secure permission to speak, and may thereby allow you to rein in their comments. Sit across from the quieter members, recognizing that when you look across the room for responses, you're more likely to catch their eye and nonverbally invite them to contribute to the discussion.

MAKE SEATING ARRANGEMENTS WORK

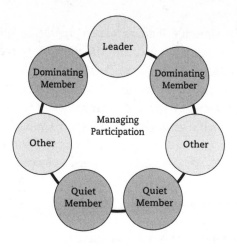

ENCOURAGE MORE PARTICIPATION IN LARGE GROUPS

It's harder to avoid making eye contact in smaller groups, which often increases participation. Studies show that participation is close to equal in a group of three (roughly divided 30/30/40 percent). But with each additional group member, participation does not necessarily remain equal. Many small group leaders can attest that in larger groups, dominating members are more likely to emerge and quieter members are more able to hide. So what can you do about that?

Consider breaking up into smaller discussion groups of 2–4 people for a portion of your discussion time. Some people may feel more comfortable sharing in smaller groups, and this gets more people talking (albeit all at once). As an added benefit, smaller groups will decrease the influence of a dominating member, and in the company of fewer members, a dominating member may become more aware of his or her contributions, or at least more aware of others' lack thereof.

BE PURPOSEFUL AND FLEXIBLE, ALL AT THE SAME TIME

Our study found several shared behaviors among the leaders of the most effective groups. Here are a few commonalities worth sharing:

The most effective leaders asked operating questions—in other words, questions that clarify the purpose of the discussion or the group. In order for this to work, both the leader and the group members must know the purpose of the discussion and the group. Members' engagement in and understanding of the purpose both permits and encourages the leader to step in. For example:

> *"Remember, this study is all about how we approach money and wealth. In light of this purpose, how does this passage . . ."*

The most effective leaders refocused their groups back to their purpose when needed. Group discussions often get off track.

Members pursue tangential topics, or a difficult member may need to be corralled. One way to get your group back on topic is to say,

> *"These are very interesting thoughts. Perhaps we can talk more about this after prayer tonight? Getting back to the text . . ."*

The most effective leaders didn't immediately answer their own questions. Inevitably, you'll ask a question that doesn't generate much interest or engagement. If this happens, work hard to resist the temptation to answer it yourself. Get comfortable with silence! If necessary, consider rephrasing the question or, even better, say to the group,

> *"Maybe I didn't ask the best question. Does anyone understand what I was going for and could maybe rephrase it?"*

The most effective leaders were willing to throw out their plan and well-crafted questions in favor of meeting a group need or an individual member's need. In Courtney's small group a few years ago, a member appeared fairly withdrawn during discussions and then stopped coming altogether. Courtney texted her a couple of times, without any response, then finally connected with her by phone. During this conversation, the group member shared that there was so much going on with her family that it was hard for her to engage and even more difficult to succinctly share a prayer request. Courtney invited her to share what was going on more fully with the whole group at the next meeting. She was honored and accepted the opportunity. This change of plan benefited the entire group. Don't be so beholden to your plan that you ignore the Spirit's leading. If you find yourself in this situation, you can say something like,

> *"Let's press pause on our study for a few minutes. Fernando, it seems like there's something on your mind. Are you willing to share more about it now or after prayer tonight?"*

Or,

> *"Nora, that took a lot of courage for you to share. You are going through a difficult time, and I'd like to pause and have our group pray with you. Would that be OK?"*

TAKE STOCK AND FOLLOW UP

You can ask the best questions, design your group's interactions with great intentionality, and copy the best leaders, but even after you do all that, you're not done leading your group's discussion. It's now time to review how the discussion went in your last meeting and prepare for the next one.

AFTER THE MEETING

First, debrief what just happened. Take lots of notes about what worked and what didn't. Debrief with co-leaders or apprentices. Schedule times for you to pray over specific members. Use reminders to follow up with group members.

Then, follow up. Maintain connection during the "other 165.75." Use your notes and call, text, or email individual members throughout the week. Ask questions in such a way that members know you care. Try to draw on specific details. For instance, rather than asking, *"How is your week going?"* try, *"How did that meeting go with your boss?"* Or instead of texting, *"Praying for you!"* pray through the text message:

> *Lord, please let Samantha know that she is seen by you during her classroom observation today. I pray that you would allow your light to shine through Samantha's hard work, expertise, and care for her students, and give Samantha supernatural peace, resting in the truth that your evaluation is the only one that matters.*

BEFORE YOUR NEXT MEETING

Prepare for good discussions. Write out a couple of guiding questions that will provide some structure for your discussion time. Using the guidelines above, consider preparing questions and question order beforehand. This can give you confidence. You'll head into the meeting knowing you have a plan, and it can help remind you where you'd like the discussion to go.

Then, prime your group members. Do you dread icebreakers that come out of nowhere? We do.

If you could have any superpower, what would it be?
If you could only eat one type of food for the rest of your life, what would it be?

Many people are indecisive or internal processors, and prefer lots of time to consider options. When a leader lobs a question like these, many people want to run and hide. If there are questions you would like group members to come prepared to answer, send them ahead of time via email or text message. This will help the internal processors to prepare something to contribute. Some examples:

For our next meeting, view the sermon online if you missed Sunday's message, and come prepared with your biggest takeaway.
We'll be talking about biblical conflict resolution. For the first question of the night, what did you and your siblings fight about the most?

KEEP THE MAIN THING THE MAIN THING

Purpose should drive your group's discussion and time together. As your group's leader, it's up to you to lead robust, purpose-driven discussions that contribute to members' spiritual growth. To take your group to the next level, learn how and prepare to ask better questions, strategically orchestrate seating arrangements, and continually review and hone your group gatherings. As you do, your group meetings will shift from trivial to transformative and spur the kind of spiritual growth that exemplifies thriving small groups.

GUEST COMMENTARY

Nearness and Racial Reconciliation

Natasha Sistrunk Robinson

The work of reconciliation looks different for each of us. For me, an African American female, it began in the professional arena when I served as the diversity outreach officer in the U.S. Naval Academy Office of Admissions. It continued when my family and I landed in a church where we were ethnic minorities. Proximity—the desire to get close—is the reason I have invested more than a decade in local congregations that are predominantly white, even in a multiethnic church. The commitment to God's diverse church has been both a challenge and a risk my family has willingly taken for the sake of the gospel.

African American author and former professor Patricia Raybon has taken the same risk. In her acclaimed book *My First White Friend* she wrote, "That is why I teach white students. To close the distance. I want to get close enough to the people I've feared and envied and hated, because nearness has a funny way of dispelling old demons."⁵ If we are building for a new way of life, then we all need to make moves.

Nearness and proximity are the first relational steps that allow us to move toward reconciliation. I'm praying that those relational moves will also challenge us to act justly and address the communal sin that's evident in our nation's systemic injustices. Without intentional and consistent action, the church lacks credibility on this topic. Conversations about racial reconciliation that exclude actionable steps toward racial injustice fall short of God's kingdom mission.

I've learned that extending forgiveness requires that I remain close to white people. I don't just mean being polite, politically correct, or tolerant. I mean being my full self in the presence of white folk—being a friend, a peacemaker, a truth teller, and a bridge builder while challenging each of us to love well, consider the other as we all grow in knowledge, and pursue higher standards for right speech and right action. We all need to get closer.

Mary was the first woman who intentionally discipled me. She was an older white woman, a former nurse, a devoted wife, and a stay-at-home mom. Mary and I had many personality differences, but we continued in our relationship by embracing unity or oneness in our diversity. Because we were both a part of God's family, we took the risk and confronted our fears. We asked each other difficult questions and did not shy away from conflict. We didn't try to pretend that we were blind to "color" or that our racial or ethnic heritage did not influence the way we read Scripture, voted, or viewed the world. We weren't afraid to share our emotional baggage and how our different social and economic experiences shaped us. We were different, and that was OK. In fact, it was good and necessary for our growth and for our service to the church. Because we were willing to push through our areas of discomfort in spite of our differences, God stretched us individually, and we are both better as a result. Mary changed the way I saw the world, and I influenced the way she viewed others who did not share her experiences.

Engaging across racial, ethnic, generational, and socioeconomic lines influences the way we experience God and love others. We make relationship commitments that require us to embrace people as God does and welcome diverse relationships that reflect true unity in the body of Christ. When we learn to love those who are different from us, we begin to see beyond ourselves and through the eyes of Jesus instead.

Church small groups are just the place to do that—to be my full self in the presence of others being their full selves, with a shared commitment to growing one another's relationships with God. Through love, compassion, curiosity, and the knowledge of God's grace, we can ask bold questions, share stories, and truly learn from each other.

Natasha Sistrunk Robinson is an international speaker, leadership consultant, and author of *A Sojourner's Truth: Choosing Freedom and Courage in a Divided World* and *Mentor for Life*. Connect at NatashaSRobinson.com. Excerpts from *A Sojourner's Truth* and *Mentor for Life* used by permission.

KEY TAKEAWAYS: HOW TO SHIFT FROM *TRIVIAL TO TRANSFORMATIVE* DISCUSSIONS IN DIFFERENT GROUP SEASONS

WHEN LAUNCHING A NEW GROUP

1. Consider the optimal seating arrangement for your group.
2. Prep for your next gathering by praying and having a game plan for the discussion.
3. Note that you will set engagement expectations for the group in the first few meetings, so begin with a bang and model the kind of behavior you wish to see.
4. Identify those who like to talk more than others. Prime the quieter ones during the week with a text or an interaction that prepares them for the next gathering.
5. Identify the common question pitfalls you are prone to commit.

WHEN MAINTAINING A GROUP'S MOMENTUM AND EFFECTIVENESS

1. Ask your group members to facilitate discussion (but before they do, ask them to read this chapter, or at least give them the back-pocket guide for questions).
2. Introduce a question that takes the group a bit deeper.
3. Follow up with each member during the week about a specific discussion point from the last group gathering.
4. Choose a couple of group members and debrief your last gathering. From their feedback, glean ways to enhance the next discussion.
5. Identify the common question pitfalls you are prone to commit.

WHEN YOUR GROUP IS STRUGGLING

1. Switch up seating arrangements. Find a way to playfully mix up the "normal" arrangement.
2. Redesign your group interactions by utilizing the inverted funnel learning process.
3. Identify the dominant talkers and the quieter ones, then prime the quieter ones with questions ahead of time.
4. Consider sub-groups for your next discussion and either putting the talkative people together or spreading them out.
5. Analyze how often your group gets off-topic during discussion, and utilize the refocusing techniques.
6. Choose a group member or two and debrief your last gathering, paying particular attention to their feedback about the quality of the discussion.

REFLECTION AND DISCUSSION QUESTIONS

Note the inverted funnel sequence. In fact, we've been using it throughout the book for these questions at the end of each chapter.

1. 👆**Remember:** What caught your attention in this chapter about stimulating better discussions?
2. 🦉**Understand:** What do you now understand about the kinds of questions that are likely to produce the best discussions?
3. ⚙️**Apply:** How might you apply this new understanding about questions and seating arrangements in your next group gathering?
4. 🔍**Analyze:** After completing the Two-Minute Tip asking a group member to write down all of the questions you asked during the group discussion, what did you learn about your tendencies?
5. 📋**Evaluate:** What adjustments might you make, now that you're aware of your inclinations?
6. 💡**Create:** What question(s) can be your new "go-to" when you sense the discussion is falling flat?
7. 💡**Create:** Name the individuals in your group whose participation you'd want to help catalyze (either more or less participation!). In your group discussions, where would you seat them? Draw it out!

CHAPTER 8

AVOIDANCE TO EMBRACE

Engage Difficult Conversations without Destroying Your Group

When you have to have that conversation,
it's hard, but worth it.

—BRAD, A SMALL GROUP LEADER

Several weeks into their group term, Lena learned from some group members that Sarah, one of the more vocal members of the group, was making some inappropriate relationship decisions. Suddenly, Lena was thrust into the mess and, as the leader of her group, needed to figure out what to do next.

If you were in Lena's shoes, what would you do? Would you ignore the situation for fear that confronting Sarah might blow up your relationship or the group? Would you confront her in a group meeting or individually? What would you say, where would you meet, and what approach would you take? How would you speak the truth in love? After all, it's not just *what* Lena does, a lot hinges on *how* she approaches this situation.

Lena thought and prayed, and prayed some more. Then she sent Sarah a text message to see if she'd be willing to meet her for coffee before work one morning. When they met, Lena raised the issue and asked the Holy Spirit to guide her words so that she would not be perceived as judgmental. They had a good, productive conversation.

Though she could not recall exactly what she said, Lena remembers that Sarah thanked her for initiating the conversation. Lena's willingness to step toward tension and not away from it showed her commitment to Sarah. Sarah felt loved and cared for. And she's still part of the group today!

Lena entered the confrontation zone, knowing that she could leverage the tension for good, both in Sarah's life and in her group. But that isn't how many leaders deal with tension-filled situations. Too often, when a difficult issue surfaces, leaders adopt a "hear-no-evil, see-no-evil" approach. They ignore the controversial statement, make an awkward joke to lighten the mood, apply a proof-texted verse to the matter, immediately set the record straight as they provide the "correct" answer, hope and pray that the issue resolves itself, or otherwise sweep the troublesome issue under the table.

What do *you* do?

Catalytic leaders are willing to have difficult conversations, at both the group level and the individual level, with loving refinement as the primary aim, because they know they are necessary and beneficial to their group's growth and individuals' growth.

Initiating challenging conversations is challenging. When you enter the confrontation zone, you move into a seemingly endless territory of multilayered, sophisticated, interpersonal land mines that have massive potential for turning into dysfunctional communication and for the destruction of relationships, maybe even the destruction of your group. Missteps in engaging the situation could result in conflict that can't be resolved.

Too often when good-hearted, well-intentioned leaders bring up difficult issues, conversations that are meant to be loving devolve into conflicts that erupt or result in alienated relationships. But it doesn't have to be that way. You can learn to engage difficult conversations without destroying your group, and leverage tension in both individual and group settings to promote growth within your group.

CATALYTIC LEADERS *EMBRACE DIFFICULT CONVERSATIONS*

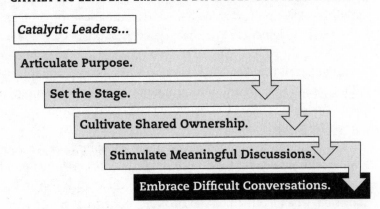

In this chapter, we want to help you see how leveraging tension and leaning into conflict has the potential to powerfully influence your small group members and learn how to navigate those difficult conversations and manage the conflict that may arise as you do.

THE POWER OF PUSHBACK

Resistance—pushback—is an essential element of life. Your muscles require resistance to grow. In the market, resistance to paying $15 for a tomato makes salsa affordable. In school, challenging feedback from teachers pushes us to become better thinkers and writers. In every area of life, we benefit from pushback.

So it is with personal and group growth. From the review of group development theory in chapter 3, you might remember the vital role conflict plays in helping a group progress to a stage wherein it can accomplish its mission. Similarly, resistance in work, in relationships, and in finances helps individuals grow into the people God has designed them to be. When confronted with challenges, people are forced to respond and make a choice, often towards or away from growth.

Conflict is one way people commonly experience resistance. Many people think of conflict predominantly as something negative they should try to avoid, but when you understand the power of pushback, you realize the goodness, utility, and potential of properly engaged conflict.

Conflict can be and often is a good thing. Interestingly, there's not always agreement on what conflict looks like or feels like. For example, we inquired about various components of conflict in our study. One question asked whether conflict had happened within the small group. Fascinatingly, not all members within the same group indicated that conflict had occurred.

In some cases, group members said a conflict had occurred in the group, but their leaders did not. Apparently, conflict can be hard to identify.

In the midst of these varying perspectives however, we found a recurring theme: the more group members reported that conflict occurred in their groups, the more the group contributed to individuals' spiritual health. Counterintuitive, right?

The more group members reported that conflict occurred in their groups, the more the group contributed to individuals' spiritual health.

Well, not quite as counterintuitive as you may think. Even though it rarely feels good in the moment, we know that conflict often spurs positive outcomes. Here are a few ways it does this:

- **Conflict can produce better understanding of both issues and people.** In the event of a disagreement, the parties involved are called to articulate their perspectives and, if this is done well, both parties gain clarity. Disagreement fosters learning.
- **Conflict can increase member motivation.** When group members participate in a conflict, they become actively involved with an issue. People who don't care will not expend energy disagreeing.
- **Conflict can produce greater cohesiveness among group members.** When conflict is resolved successfully, members learn that the ties holding the group together are strong enough to withstand disagreement. Conflict can serve to strengthen the bonds between us.

So the most effective groups fight more?

Sort of, but not exactly. Of course, unresolved, pervasive conflict can have negative effects, but in the most effective groups in our study, members reported conflict. Furthermore, groups that experienced conflict and developed norms for how to communicate and approach future conflict contributed more to their members' spiritual growth than those that experienced less conflict and did not establish communicative norms for dealing with conflict when it occurs. This means the groups that were willing to "go there," to push back on one another, and to increase tension rather than run from it had a greater impact on their members' growth than groups that didn't.

Here's the key takeaway: when your group members are willing to push back on one another, even if conflict occurs, and your group is able to work through it, growth often results. So lean into conflict rather than flee from it. Members in top groups reported that their leaders were able to facilitate quality discussions, engage in active listening, and say hard things when needed. That sounds a lot like being able to engage challenging conversations and channel the power of pushback effectively.

> When your group members are willing to push back on one another, even if conflict occurs, and your group is able to work through it, growth often results.

If you tend to ignore or squash potential conflict, we encourage you to rethink the power of increasing and leveraging tension for the good of your group. Resist the urge to minimize tension in your group, and be willing to strategically, yet diplomatically, increase tension. The power of pushback just might be what your group needs in order to fulfill its mission.

LEAN INTO, NOT AWAY FROM, TENSION

If handled well, tension can be a tool to propel your group's spiritual growth. Now, we don't encourage you to go looking for conflict, but when it comes around, you need to lean in and try to turn it into something productive. The best leaders take a thoughtful approach that walks the tightrope of tension and finds a way to leverage the moment.

Take Tom, for instance. Tom leads a small group in a Midwestern church. One day, he received a call from Phil, a member of his small group, who had just been arrested for driving under the influence. He was in the clink, and Tom was his one phone call. Tom was shocked. Phil had been sober for almost eight months and was seemingly doing well, and his small group was a key part of his journey. So when Phil called, Tom wanted to love Phil well while also navigating the situation with his group. Tom knew he would need to engage individually with Phil on some issues (with the help of his pastor or a counselor) but also lead the group to respond and care well for Phil. He quickly realized that he didn't really know how to handle things, but a number of people would be looking to him for direction because the dynamics of the group had just changed.

You might think that this could never happen to you and your group. But stranger things have happened, and this situation illustrates the complexity leaders must address when challenging situations arise. Put yourself in Tom's shoes for a second. How would you support Phil? What role should the rest of the small group play? What role should you play? Now, let's go a bit further. How much do you know about recovery support? Who else might you need to know about this situation?

Luckily, several principles can help pave the way forward. These four responses can set the stage for how you can leverage tension for the good of the members you lead and your group as a whole.

TAKE TIME TO PRAY AND IDENTIFY WHAT'S REALLY GOING ON.

Pause. Pray. Ask God to give you the ability to see what is really happening and how you might proceed.

ACKNOWLEDGE YOUR OWN CAPACITY, STRENGTHS, AND LIMITATIONS.

No one is perfect, including you. As a human being, you have a limited capacity to manage difficult situations, and that capacity often changes. Tense moments can stir up past situations that were personally polarizing. They have a way of blurring relationship lines and breaking apart years of seemingly sturdy connections with others. Such moments may tempt you to make quick, uninformed judgments as to who or what is right. Thus, it is so important for you to be honest with yourself so that you can be honest with those around you.

CONSULT OTHERS WHO CAN PROVIDE YOU WITH HELPFUL RESOURCES.

Pay attention to what you are actually capable of handling, and quickly acknowledge when something is "above your pay grade." Tom realized he needed additional input, so he connected with his small group coach, the small group staff, and counselors at his church. These staff members and trusted counselors helped Tom learn how to pursue, love, and support everyone in his group. Don't be afraid to reach out for help when you're in over your head.

DETERMINE HOW MUCH THE SITUATION IS A "GROUP THING" VERSUS AN "INDIVIDUAL THING."

Reduce the number of people who need to be involved to the smallest number that can adequately provide the resources necessary to help. Determine who needs to be, *not wants to be*, a part of the resolution process. Is this an individual situation, or should it involve *multiple group members*? If multiple members need to be involved, then it's also important to identify exactly how they should be involved. Pray that God will help you discern this. Because the group had already walked with Phil through his situation over the past many months, Tom considered how much he should involve his group members with the initial care and support for Phil. He concluded that he, his coleader, and Phil would be the smallest circle, and the rest of the group would be "in the know" but not bogged down with the gritty details. In this way, Tom freed his group to provide support and establish a safe environment for Phil without being unnecessarily involved.

Although uncomfortable, Tom resolved to lean into and leverage the tension he and his group would face and strategically approached it.

LEVERAGE CONFRONTATION

Once you've determined your initial responses, it's time to seize the moment. The following four actions will help you leverage confrontation for positive growth:

CONSIDER HOW RESOLVING THE CURRENT CONFLICT WILL IMPROVE HOW THE INDIVIDUALS AND THE GROUP WILL INTERACT IN THE FUTURE.

How you engage conflict will, right or wrong, model your own desired approach toward future conflict. If group members can hear and see how conflict can be resolved in a healthy way, they might approach their own conflicts differently. Don't wait for conflict to arise before you start modeling healthy interaction.

As a leader, you can prepare group members for conflict by examining how Scripture approaches this subject. Matthew 18:15–17 and Galatians 6:1 provide excellent case studies on how to prepare for conflict. Taking an objective look at healthy ways to approach conflict can help move a group from peacekeeping to peacemaking. In our view, the main difference is that *peacemaking* actively involves all members of a group, whereas *peacekeeping* primarily involves policing by the leader.

A *peacekeeping* group is primarily preoccupied with compliance, and a lot of effort is placed on maintaining the status quo. Like siblings who run to a parent at the first sign of conflict, group members' heads will swivel to the leader to see how he or she is going to handle things. In this scenario, group members assume their leader will have the final say. In the end, *peacekeeping* deals mostly with self-preservation. This approach teaches members that personal avoidance and deferring to the leader is the best approach.

Conversely, a *peacemaking* group is primarily preoccupied with genuineness and forthrightness. Thus, great effort is placed on candor. Like good diplomats gathering together to come to a working resolution, group members bring their best efforts and aspire to become a group wherein everyone understands and owns their responsibilities. A *peacemaking* approach promotes the idea that "honesty is the best policy."

TWO-MINUTE TIP

Invite two trusted group members to read this chapter and set up a time to talk about how leveraging conflict and tension can contribute to your group's stated purpose. Then, invite them to lean into future tension with you.

In our study, we found that groups who took time to establish boundaries, determine and model how to appropriately interact with each other, and provide accountability whenever those boundary markers were broken had a more robust group experience. They were *peacemaking* groups.

Once confrontation has occurred, establishing the end goal helps set in motion the course of action that will follow. Similar to stating the purpose for your group gatherings, you forecast what life will look like once a particular conflict has been successfully resolved.

ENGAGE THE INDIVIDUAL WITH A BALANCE OF GRACE AND TRUTH, AND MANAGE GROUP BOUNDARIES.

Approach each group member with the same grace and truth you would desire or require for yourself, with love covering all. In the example of Tom and Phil, Tom was able to forecast a plan of action that set boundaries for healthy interactions with the group, and which helped provide accountability for his group member in need. With Phil's permission, Tom identified which people would be involved. Tom determined he and his co-leader would be best suited to primarily help Phil. Tom then identified some healthy, supportive, and secondary roles his group members could fill, such as sending encouraging texts, sitting together during Sunday services, and including Phil in social gatherings.

SET A TIME TO GATHER AND PREPARE EVERYONE FOR THE DIRECTION YOU ALL WILL GO.

The goal is to journey in and through conflict. Establishing a date, time, and location tangibly helps get the ball rolling. Along with setting logistics, sending questions for each person to think about repositions everyone to be able to find resolutions as opposed to trying to find who is *right*. Much like crafting good questions for small group discussion, you as a leader have an opportunity to refocus individuals and group members on the ultimate goal: reconciliation. Conversation starters like the following can carve a roadmap toward resolution:

> *What is the main conflict?*
> *What do I need to take responsibility for in this conflict?*
> *When I think about our relationship, what am I most*
>   *concerned about?*
> *What am I most willing to do?*

FOLLOW THROUGH TOWARD RESOLUTION.

A critical but often overlooked initial step in leveraging tension is helping group members go from facing each other to facing the problem at hand. For example, Tom helped group members understand that Phil's issue was not between group members but rather an opportunity for group members to rally around Phil. Tom modeled to the entire group how to do this. His modeling provided clarity to the group and necessary support for Phil.

As Tom maneuvered through the details of helping his group member, he and his coleader took the time to learn what helpful, healthy, and accountable interactions would look like for his group members. By consulting with his coach, the small group staff, and counselors at his church, Tom was able to forecast a plan of action that gave boundaries for healthy interactions with all of his group members moving forward and that helped provide accountability for his member in need.

TIPS FOR MANAGING SEVEN PARTICULARLY CHALLENGING GROUP MEMBERS

The sheer nature of gathering a diverse group of people almost ensures that you will encounter one or more of the following personalities. Though you may be tempted to avoid or sideline the issues these personalities invite, we suggest you tackle them head-on. Transformational opportunities lie in wait as you do. Here, we list several common types of group members, and then offer several strategies to productively engage each one.

SOMEONE WHO DOMINATES DISCUSSION

There are a number of ways to handle the conversation monopolizer. First, before your next group gathering, ask the group member to wait to verbally contribute until three or four other members have talked. For example, "Your contributions are so valuable to the group, and it's clear it's easy for you to respond, but it isn't easy for everyone. Can you help me get others to participate more by stepping back so they have to step up?" Second, structure your dialogue by going around the circle clockwise or counterclockwise and asking everyone to contribute in that order. Third, invite the monopolizer to help you invite others into the conversation. "Johnny, have you noticed that Rodrigo doesn't usually say much in the discussion? Would you help me encourage him to speak up more? Maybe you could meet up with him to find out how we can best engage him?" Finally, use the diagram in the last chapter to make seating arrangements work. Sit next to the dominator and make eye contact with other members after you ask a question.

SOMEONE WHO DOESN'T PARTICIPATE

Before your next group gathering, meet with this group member and ask how small group is helping them grow. You could encourage them to participate by highlighting times when their participation positively contributed to the group. For instance, "Olivia, when you speak, the rest of the group listens intently. They respect what you have to contribute. I encourage you to speak up more in group." Alternatively, you could break the group into smaller groups of three or four members, which may help introverted members feel more comfortable.

SOMEONE WHO IS OVERLY NEEDY

Set up a time outside of the group gathering to connect with this person. Consider encouraging another group member to reach out and make a connection as well. This is a great way to invite members into deeper engagement in the group. Remember, by devoting too much group time to this person, you might ignore other people's needs, prompting them to seek the support they need elsewhere.

SOMEONE WHO IS TOO TASK-ORIENTED

Consider affirming this person's focus by asking this group member to facilitate a portion of the group gathering that feels more operational in nature. Then, take some time to cast a vision for the parts of your gatherings that seem unimportant to this member, and ask this person to contribute fully during those times, as well.

SOMEONE WHO CONSTANTLY BLAMES OTHERS

This one is difficult and requires some contextual understanding. It's likely a one-on-one conversation will be a good starting place. Ask this person to consider taking responsibility for various conflicts or challenges.

SOMEONE WHO RARELY SHOWS UP

Meet with the group member individually and ask if this season still works for them to participate. If you sense the group member is looking to get out, provide a gracious exit opportunity. Otherwise, cast a vision for continued participation in the group, and encourage the group member to make it to the next gathering.

SOMEONE WHO DRAGS THE GROUP DOWN WITH GRUMPINESS

Initiate a conversation to help the member understand his or her impact on the group, then ask that member to use his or her influence for positive effect. It would be worth connecting with the person individually and figuring out what is contributing to his or her grumpiness. You never know what might be just below the surface.

WHEN CONFLICT EMERGES IN YOUR GROUP

At this point, you might think we've covered everything possible about conflict and confrontation.

Whenever people gather together, choose to be open and transparent, and are willing to lean into and leverage tension, the potential for group conflict dramatically increases. Thus, when developing the kind of groups we're talking about here—healthy groups that promote spiritual growth—the issue really isn't a matter of if, but *when*, conflict will occur. Often that conflict will seem to come out of nowhere. Engage these seven strategies to manage conflict well when it unexpectedly arises in your group:

> **Relax.** People's points of view on important topics are shaped by differing (usually taken-for-granted) values, belief systems, and interests. Conflict is bound to surface, so don't freak out.
>
> **Acknowledge the "elephant in the room."** Pause the conversation to address tension or awkwardness when a conversation crosses the line.
>
> **Pay attention to your emotions and the emotions of others.** Allow yourself and your group members to express what they're feeling and why. Treat one another's feelings and perspectives as legitimate topics of concern and conversation.

Consider alternative interpretations. If you are offended by what someone has said, be willing to offer their alternative interpretation the benefit of the doubt.

Determine the best time to engage the conflict. If the conflict can be resolved quickly and fully, engage it and get back to your group's discussion. If it's going to take a while, don't sweep the conflict under the rug, but realize the timing might not be right to address it.

Work it out fully. If the conflict is not resolved quickly, work it out fully in individual conversations with the persons involved until they can come to a place of reconciliation.

Learn from it. Take some time in your next group gathering (or sooner, if necessary) to revisit the conflict. Ask all members for their thoughts and feelings about the conflict. Discuss what your group can learn from it, and consider what it looks like to love and respect one another as brothers and sisters in Christ. Talk about how you can best engage together in the future. When relevant, capture what you learned by revising and re-signing your group's covenant.

TWO-MINUTE TIP

As you review the list above about how to manage conflict well, underline or highlight the strategy you'd like to pursue next time. Take a picture of it and send it to another group member, asking that person to help you accomplish your goal.

LEAN IN AND LEAD FORWARD

When you leverage tension and manage conflict well, you model the usefulness of conflict. You guide members to see the usefulness of conflict, engage the mess, and then work through it. After all, that's what we hope groups will do! One of the major reasons for engaging healthy group development and facilitating robust group discussions is to set the stage for the ugly and the mess. This is what groups are for!

Imagine how dynamic your group will be if it learns how to lean into tension and journey through conflict in a healthy fashion. How might relationships outside your group change once your members begin to model for others how to navigate and leverage difficult situations? Most importantly, how might your group radically change the world around it and point others toward Jesus through healthy conflict?

GUEST COMMENTARY

LEARNING TO HEAR ONE ANOTHER

Amy Jackson

I had no idea that talking about emotions could erupt into such a polarizing conversation. During a recent small group, which I led, we were discussing Peter Scazzero's book *Emotionally Healthy Spirituality*. The conversation had two particular group members up in arms—and on opposite sides. Scazzero writes, "God intends that we mature in learning to recognize how he speaks and guides us through our feelings." [1] I read the quote, opened it up for discussion, and immediately felt the tension in the room. One group member nodded emphatically, all but jumping up and down in agreement, commenting on how this was completely true. She had a background in counseling ministry, and she started dropping names of studies and experts to make her point that emotions should guide us, seeing them as a way that God speaks to us. And then she dropped this bomb: "I can't believe anyone could think differently!"

At the same time, another group member was growing visibly frustrated. She crossed her arms in front of her, and her lips formed a thin line of disapproval. It appeared she might literally be biting her tongue to keep herself from interrupting. As soon as there was a break in the discussion, she quickly piped up, saying, "I don't believe this at all. In fact, this kind of talk can cause a lot of damage." She elaborated by sharing about some negative family experiences with counseling that had led her to believe all emotion-talk was hogwash. In fact, she believed that, as Christians, we need to learn to ignore our emotions because they will lead us astray.

The two stared each other down, and the rest of the group grew uncomfortably quiet.

As the group facilitator, I needed to create an environment for open, thoughtful, and respectful conversation. Clearly there were different opinions present, and they both had some validity. I had my own strong opinions on the topic, and I felt them bubbling up inside of me, but I actively set them aside to help us truly discuss the topic *with* one another rather than speak opinions *at* each other. Engaging difficult conversations requires that we each listen fully to the other person—not to come up with our own rebuttal, or so that we can immediately correct them, but so we can *understand* them. In general, people make decisions and believe things for a reason, and we have to begin with this grace-filled stance.

This kind of conversation opens the group to something incredibly meaningful: feeling seen, heard, and understood. We all want to be seen and understood whole people, and yet it's often scary to allow others to see who we truly are. We don't need everyone to agree with us or come to the same conclusions, but we crave people who can truly show empathy for our situation, decisions, and thoughts. This is something that engaging conflict in small groups can do for group members—and it's why engaging conflict can be truly transformational. If we can leave the discussion knowing that others saw and understood us, even if we still disagree, we feel bonded in a unique way.

To help guide us toward empathetic discussion, I thanked both women for sharing and affirmed that they both had valid reasons to believe what they did. "I know I was personally taught that emotions weren't to be trusted at all, and that there were certain emotions that were off-limits completely—like anger. After all, we don't want to sin because we're being guided by strong emotions," I shared. "Through the years, though, I've realized that even Jesus sometimes exhibited anger in healthy and helpful ways, so I wonder if our emotions can guide us toward what God wants us to do—at least some of the time. What do the rest of you think?"

It opened discussion to both sides of the conversation, as well as a middle ground, and it welcomed other group members to share their thoughts. I used statements like, "Help us understand what led you to that place," and "I can definitely understand how you ended up there." This probing and affirming helped us understand not only *what* people thought, but *why* they thought it. We were truly seeking to understand. We agreed to continue thinking about both sides of the conversation throughout the week, and to pay attention to our own emotions. When we gathered again, we all had a better understanding of the conversation, and we had more empathy for other views. This reminded us that we truly can and should learn from others, especially those who see things differently from us. At the end of the group, the two women who had started on opposite sides started meeting one-on-one, all on their own, to continue learning from one another. By engaging the conflict, they felt bonded rather than further apart.

Amy Jackson is founder and director of The Perch, which provides space and skills for soul care. She is a former publisher for church resources at *Christianity Today*, including SmallGroups .com. Connect on Twitter @AmyKJackson.

KEY TAKEAWAYS: HOW TO SHIFT FROM *AVOIDANCE TO EMBRACE* IN DIFFERENT GROUP SEASONS

WHEN LAUNCHING A NEW GROUP
1. Study the peacemaking passages as a group, and discuss perceived approaches to future conflict.
2. Review the tips for managing challenging people, and identify which ones you might need extra help with.
3. Involve the group in planning how you will handle future conflict.
4. Set boundaries and expectations for ways to leverage tension well.

WHEN MAINTAINING A GROUP'S MOMENTUM AND EFFECTIVENESS
1. Identify your group as either peacemakers or peacekeepers, then study the differences together.
2. Familiarize yourself with the 7 strategies for managing conflict well.
3. Utilize the tips for challenging people section. Have fun with this and see if your group can identify each other or themselves in this list.

WHEN YOUR GROUP IS STRUGGLING
1. Identify your group as either peacemaking or peacekeeping.
2. Spend time individually with the pre-discussion prompts for the leader (see the end of the chapter).
3. Carefully identify conflict in your group and utilize the pre-discussion prompts for your group to flesh this out.
4. Utilize the tips for managing particularly challenging people.

REFLECTION AND DISCUSSION QUESTIONS

PRE-DISCUSSION REFLECTION PROMPTS:
How do you typically approach conflict?

1. Do you, as the leader, confront members who don't contribute to the group?

2. Do you have ground rules about speaking the truth in love that set up group members to interact well with each other?

3. Do you hold group members accountable when they violate these rules?

4. As a leader, do you clarify important issues and perspectives, even if it might create an awkward moment?

5. When conflict rears its ugly head, do you immediately try to squelch it or let it linger?

6. When things get out of hand within your group, do you spend time in prayer?

How has your group previously dealt with conflict?

1. Has your group embraced conflict or shut it down?
2. When arguments have occurred, have group members initially used descriptive evidence, or have they initially expressed feelings?
3. In what ways have group members been held accountable by other group members?
4. When have you seen group members say hard things, even if it has resulted in awkwardness or conflict?

DISCUSSION QUESTIONS:

1. What did God reveal to you through the reflection prompts?
2. If "conflict" and "tension" were people, what three words might you use to describe your relationship with them?
3. **Remember:** What caught your attention in this chapter about leveraging tension and engaging conflict?
4. **Understand:** What do you now understand about the benefits of conflict?
5. **Apply:** What might it look like to determine how much a situation is a "group thing" or an "individual thing"?
6. **Analyze:** Is there a particular issue that you "buried" (or was buried by the group leader) in a previous group experience? What happened, and what was the result?
7. **Evaluate:** Consider the last time you experienced conflict within a small group. What did you learn from it? How did it help or hurt your group? In which areas might you ask the Lord to help you grow?
8. **Create:** What are the first three things you want to think about or do the next time you sense tension?

PART 3

THREE ESSENTIAL DISCIPLINES TO SUSTAIN YOUR LONG-TERM EFFECTIVENESS

Reaching the promised land is possible. But you must take careful care of yourself.

As you continue to lead from a place of health, your leadership should expand to recruit and train those within your group for leadership. Before you know it, your group will be ready to expand and grow.

These disciplines will refresh and unleash your influence.

Chapter 9: Your Care:
Cultivating and Sustaining Your Own Health

Chapter 10: Your Legacy:
Recruiting and Raising Up New Leaders

Chapter 11: Your Charge:
Expanding and Multiplying Groups

Chapter 12: Your Best Next Step

CHAPTER 9

YOUR CARE

Cultivating and Sustaining Your Own Health

*For no good tree bears bad fruit, nor again does a bad
tree bear good fruit, for each tree is known by its own
fruit. For figs are not gathered from thornbushes, nor
are grapes picked from a bramble bush. The good person
out of the good treasure of his heart produces good, and
the evil person out of his evil treasure produces evil, for
out of the abundance of the heart his mouth speaks.*

—JESUS, LUKE 6:43–45

*Almost everything will work again if you
unplug it for a few minutes, including you.*

—ANNE LAMOTT

Perhaps you've only been leading a group for the last couple of
months. Perhaps you've been leading one for years. While you're
working toward your group's articulated purpose, leading great discussions, and embracing difficult conversations, you're also carrying
the emotional burden of your group members' struggles. Maybe one

of your group members is struggling with depression, which is affecting his marriage, work, and relationships with others. Maybe one of your group members has an unbelieving spouse and needs regular encouragement. Maybe one of your group members is making big decisions about a new career and geographic move, prompting prayer through relational, spiritual, and logistical challenges. Oh, and there are at least four other group members as well.

And you? Maybe you work full-time, in or out of the home, care for children or elderly parents, and volunteer with a nonprofit organization, and you deal with all the responsibilities that accompany those roles.

All of these responsibilities can take a significant toll on your emotional, physical, and spiritual well-being, and before you know it, leadership malaise can creep in. You're weary, and though you don't want to admit it, you feel the urge to leave the group and your leadership responsibilities. Things aren't what they used to be, and you begin to think that it must be time to quit. Doubts linger, you begin to notice only the negative, and you wonder what needs to give.

These are the classic signs of burnout.

But the goal isn't just to avoid burnout. Soccer players know that when they're taking a penalty kick, avoiding the goalie isn't the strategy for success. In fact, they say that if you keep your focus on the goalie, hoping to score, you'll actually kick it to her every time. Instead, players are trained to focus (covertly!) on a specific corner of the back of the net. The goal in small group leadership is spiritual and emotional self-care. In soccer, scoring a goal on a penalty kick means you've avoided the goalie. In small groups, pursuing ongoing self-care and sustainable leadership practices means you avoid burnout.

> **The majority of group members look to you as their leader to be spiritually healthy. Not perfect, but healthy.**

Our study found something simple but profound: the majority of group members look to you as their leader to be spiritually healthy. Not perfect, but healthy. This means you must take care of yourself in such a way that you can continually thrive and grow through the ups and downs of small group leadership.

Maybe you're in the middle of a storm right now. If so, it's time to exhale and examine the quality of your spiritual soil. Cultivating your spiritual soil will prepare you for the ongoing work God has for you as a leader. This chapter will help you understand your spiritual soil and identify ways you can exhale, be real, and care for yourself while continuing to sharpen your skills as a group leader.

TAKE STOCK OF YOUR SPIRITUAL SOIL

As for [seeds] in the good soil, they are those who, hearing the word, hold it fast in an honest and good heart, and bear fruit with patience. (Luke 8:15)

When Jason's friend Philip took over his family farm, he committed himself to learning the family trade. Along the way, the parable of the sower in Luke 8 became clearer to him, and in particular what makes soil good and able to produce great yields. Through his experience, Philip learned that not all soils are created equal. Some soil combinations are better and more ready for high yield than others. These soil combinations are a conglomeration of a number of controllable and uncontrollable factors that actively create a variant capacity for yields. Some soil combinations are favorable; others are unfavorable.

RECOGNIZE UNFAVORABLE CONDITIONS

Without being overly formulaic, not taking any of the actions addressed in this book can contribute to *unfavorable* conditions for your leadership and your group members' experience. In struggling groups, leaders tend to overcompensate and take on a greater role. But this calculated leadership move often has unintended outcomes:

- If your group doesn't have a compelling purpose, you may find yourself tired of trying to motivate group members and discouraged by their lack of commitment.

- If your group doesn't have a good structure for gathering, you may find yourself frustrated by the lack of predictability or meaningfulness.
- If your group members sit idly by, expecting you to do everything for them, you may find yourself exhausted from juggling all the matters of group life.
- If your group doesn't engage in meaningful discussion and conversation, you may find yourself having to pry responses from group members and questioning the worth of gathering.
- If your group avoids any and all confrontation, you may find yourself annoyed, ready to throw in the towel because no one wants to be authentic, and discouraged by the lack of evidenced spiritual growth.

And that's just the *group's* contribution to your spiritual soil. As a leader, you know your own life—the personal commitments, struggles, trials, and temptations you face daily.

It doesn't take long in life, particularly in leadership, to experience personal pain. Maybe a trusted friend suddenly turned his back on you, or you made a decision that didn't work out. Maybe you shared something in a confidential setting that was then shared with others, intentionally or unintentionally hurting a group member's feelings. Maybe you've experienced struggles with your family, or you are facing physical or mental health issues. All of these and a hundred more scenarios can cause you pain as a leader and as a person.

Left unattended, the combination of group and personal dynamics can lead to burnout.

One of the greatest biblical examples of leadership burnout comes from Exodus 18. Moses, the great leader of the nation of Israel, was visited by his father-in-law, Jethro. It was the first family gathering since the exodus from Egypt. During this family reunion, Jethro quickly noticed that Moses was cultivating unfavorable conditions in his leadership and for his people. You might say that Jethro was the first organizational consultant.

Moses' father-in-law said to him, "What you are doing is not good. You and the people with you will certainly *wear yourselves out*, for the thing is *too heavy* for you. *You are not able to do it alone*." (Ex. 18:17–18, emphasis ours)

Moses possessed great leadership skills; after all, he led an entire nation (with God's hand and help) out of slavery. And yet, even though he had perfectly good intentions, he was headed straight for disaster. His pace was not sustainable, his burdens were too much for one person, and he wasn't utilizing his resources. He wasn't allowing able people around him to take ownership and share the load. Jethro recognized that these factors were creating unfavorable conditions.

The good news is that Moses was also an attentive follower and listener: "So Moses listened to the voice of his father-in-law and did all that he had said" (Ex. 18:24).

As you reflect on Moses' example, ask yourself where you are right now. Is your current pace sustainable, or are you wearing yourself out? Are you getting enough rest, exercising regularly, and eating well? What burdens—both inside and outside your group—are too numerous or heavy for you to carry alone? Are you shouldering situations that are not yours to carry? What resources are available to you right now that you are not utilizing? Are you listening and responding to what you hear?

British pastor G. Campbell Morgan was right when he said, "[People] called by God to lead are always in danger of attempting to encompass more than they are able."[1] You get it. As a leader, you have walked the road that leads to burnout; you have felt the insurmountable and sometimes endless burdens that arise in everyday life; and you have convinced, coaxed, or Jedi-mind-tricked yourself into thinking you can handle all of it. But Jesus himself reminds us that we can't and invites us to lean into him: "Come to me, all who labor and are heavy laden, and I will give you rest" (Matt. 11:28).

When you lean into Jesus, allow him to care for your soul, and take care of yourself, you create favorable conditions for your own growth and the growth of others.

CULTIVATE FAVORABLE CONDITIONS

Nick, a groups pastor in the Northeast, articulates one of their ministry values as, "Don't do more; do better." In particular, he focuses on helping leaders take care of themselves so they can take care of their members. We trust that your ministry leaders pray often that you are strengthened and encouraged and that they are constantly trying to find ways to encourage, equip, and empower you. In fact, small groups pastors indicated to us that your spiritual growth and well-being is their number one concern.

Take Advantage of Your Protections

Before you get to the point of burnout, take some time to identify the resources—or, as we refer to them, protections—available to you. They may come in one of the following forms:

- **Resource protections.** From a leadership perspective, what training and development resources does your church or parachurch ministry offer? Take advantage of them. The leaders of the top groups in our study indicated they had engaged in significantly more training opportunities than leaders of other groups. What trainings, handbooks, leadership experiences, retreats, or opportunities are designed to help you? Among others, smallgroups.com provides a plethora of leadership tips and teachings to protect you from the pitfalls of small group leadership. More resources are listed in Appendix A.
- **Organizational protections.** Likewise, when it comes to your well-being and spiritual development, what support is available from your church or ministry in terms of mentoring, coaching, and spiritual direction? Your ministry and pastoral staff can fill this need or provide others to guide and coach your spiritual leadership development.
- **Boundary protections.** You can't do everything. And even if you think you can, you shouldn't. In noble attempts to be unselfish and caring, leaders often neglect their own limitations. Consider what you are willing to do and what you're not willing

to do, in order to steward what you're responsible for and rightfully let go of what you are not. What do you need to give up? Which relationship completely drains you? Which activity overextends you? Maybe it is time to consider what Henry Cloud calls a "necessary ending," a termination of something "whose time has passed." If this something is not ended, bad things happen, or good things don't. As Cloud rightly warns, "Without the ability to end things, people stay stuck, never becoming who they are meant to be, never accomplishing all that their talents and abilities should afford them."[2]

Without adequate resource, ministry, and boundary protections, you open yourself up to burnout, which ultimately hinders you, your group members, and the church. But with the right protections in place, you can cultivate sustainable leadership practices that propel the spread of the gospel across communities and individual hearts.

Dann Spader, a longtime disciple-maker and worldwide teacher of disciple-making practices, explains, "While we cannot make fruit happen, we can create a healthy environment for maximum growth to take place. Fruitfulness is not something we can produce. It is a by-product of abiding in the life of Jesus."[3]

Fertilize Your Soil

Although your pastors and ministry leaders care immensely about your growth, they cannot *make* you grow. In the same way that purpose is the engine that drives group growth, abiding in Jesus fuels your soul care.

Just as there are habits and behaviors that predictably contribute to leader burnout and seasons of barrenness, there are practices that create favorable conditions for ongoing leadership. We'll introduce four super-charged disciplines that will revitalize, restore, replenish, and redeem your leadership (and thankfully, none of them are cow manure).[4] At the beginning of each section, we've presented you with a question to consider before you dig deeper into that discipline.

Enjoy God's Word

When was the last time you really enjoyed and craved time in the Word?

Our study revealed that 42.5 percent of group members are in the Word of God almost every day or every other day. That leaves 57.5 percent of group members who read Scripture a few times a week or less, with 8.7 percent rarely or never spending time in the Word.

Furthermore, 53 percent of leaders surveyed were consistently in the Word in some fashion (almost every day or every day). By comparison, 17 percent of leaders reported a habit of once a week or less. And remember, these were leaders of the small groups that were considered most effective by their ministry leaders!

What is your current habit of feasting on God's Word? As a leader, are you with the 53 percent or the 17 percent? Regardless of where you are now, there are steps you can take to more fully enjoy God's Word.

First, find a place. One way to create a consistent habit is to find a location in which you feel comfortable. Aim for a place with minimal distractions and optimal opportunity for focus. Maybe it's a favorite chair, a spot in your local park, or a corner table in a local coffee shop. Wherever it is, claim a specific place for you and God's Word.

Second, choose a path. There are countless ways to study the Word. Choose a direction and go with it. Read a proverb a day, or work your way through Psalms. Or, choose a specific reading plan that helps you cover a lot of ground in the Bible. Whatever you pursue, try to get into Scripture daily.

Third, develop a process. How you engage the Word of God matters. Consider writing down key words, phrases, and thoughts as you read and interact with God's Word. Highlight any phrase, verse, or section of Scripture that jumps out at you. Make note of any memory, thought, or connection your reading prompts. Write your thoughts anywhere—in the

Bible app you use, in a document on your computer, or with a good ol' pen and paper. Return to it a few days later. If you are looking for a structured way to engage with Scripture, consider employing the "Look, Learn, Live" method:

Look: What is happening in this passage? Who are the key players? Where is this taking place?

Learn: What can I learn about Jesus and his kingdom from this passage?

Live: How can I apply this passage to my life today?

Finally, share with others. Once you have established a place, chosen a path, and developed a process, we encourage you to regularly share what are you reading and learning with at least one other person. French thinker Joseph Joubert once said, "To teach is to learn twice."[5] Sharing with others benefits you both: you solidify your learning through sharing, and others learn from your study of the Word of God.

The goal here isn't a legalistic, get-through-the-Bible-in 90-days, thump-you-over-the head-with-spiritually-shaming-data approach to Bible study. Rather, we encourage you to engage a regular rhythm of Word intake that allows the truth, life, and vitality of the Word of God to infiltrate the deepest corners and recesses of your soul. Like a leisurely summer afternoon spent tubing down a river or a good hike through the Rocky Mountains, feasting on and enjoying God's Word *revitalizes* your relationship with Jesus.

Pray with Intimacy

Is your prayer time more intimate and interactive or more tactical and transactional?

Prayer is vitally important in the personal life of a leader. Most small group leader handbooks, trainings, and coaching sessions characterize prayer as a bedrock habit for any leader who wants to follow Jesus.

Jim Egli, long-time pastor and small group expert, has under-scored the importance of an intimate prayer life for leaders. In particular, Jim's research and work with small group leaders indi-cates that your prayers and prayer life significantly impact the growth of your group. He found that leaders and groups with strong prayer lives are three times more likely to see new people come to Jesus than those that do not have strong prayer lives.[6] Our data also suggests that prayer matters. In our top twenty groups (those in which the group contributed most to individuals' spiritual growth), leaders prayed two or more times per week, whereas leaders of average groups prayed only a few times per month.

How is an intimate prayer life imperative for leader wholeness and leadership sustainability? Egli extracts four reasons:

- God answers prayer.
- Praying leaders are more compassionate.
- God directs praying leaders.
- Praying leaders invite God's presence.[7]

We add a fifth: Prayer *restores* your relationship with Jesus. Just like a good conversation with a trusted friend strengthens that friendship, prayer strengthens our relationship with Jesus.

Prayer is the single most important but often most difficult organic habit to cultivate. If, indeed, Jesus is the true vine and God is the gardener (John 15:1), then whatever fruit is produced through us, the branches, is produced through our abiding in him. When we abide in him, we know that we can do nothing apart from him, so we rest in the finished work of Christ as we continue the unfinished work he has set before us.

Jim Egli says plainly, "If you want a healthy, growing group, you need to pray. So, consistently take time with God."[8] He suggests three easy ways for leaders to pray: pray for your friends, pray for your small group gatherings and community, and pray for your individual small group members.

Mike, a small group leader in the Midwest, said it well: "My most important times as a leader are when I take time to talk with the Lord. I'm finding out that the more I shut my mouth and listen and hear [the Lord] through prayer, I am reminded more and more of who I am. I am reminded of who I am in him."

Your leadership begins and ends with prayer.

Worship with Passion

What moves you to worship with passion and intensity?

As we discussed in chapter 5, regular habits of worship within your group gatherings positively impact the spiritual growth of group members. In much the same way, personal and private worship deepen the roots of your formation. However, a majority of leaders have not developed a personal rhythm of worship. And, perhaps by extension, most groups do not spend enough time worshipping together.

Worship can be anything that captures and centers the attention of your heart, mind, and soul fully on God. Consider trying out these methods of personal worship:

- Speak the Psalms out loud.
- Listen to your favorite worship music.
- Take a walk in nature.
- Write praises to God in a journal or post on the refrigerator.
- Remember the first time you experienced Jesus.
- Recall a time you had a major decision to make and you felt the Holy Spirit prompt you in a certain way.
- Do nothing but sit and watch God working in the world.

Worship *replenishes* your relationship with Jesus. The more you intently worship, the more you experience his presence. Therefore, consider the types of musical worship that replenish your soul, how you can incorporate them into your daily rhythms more often, and the indoor and outdoor environments that provide an atmosphere of worship for you. And then, worship with passion.

TWO-MINUTE TIP

Take two minutes to put together a playlist of 3–5 songs that allow you to bask in the goodness of the gospel and God's great love for you. Then find and schedule 20–30 minutes this week to take a walk or a drive and listen to those songs on repeat.

Pursue Community Intentionally

How often do you intentionally allow people to see what's happening beneath the surface in your life?

This fourth discipline of organic self-care might make the most sense, but it also might be difficult to live out as a small group leader. Believe it or not, you need to intentionally identify your people, take your pain to them, and lean into the resources available to you. In light of Jethro's counsel to Moses in Exodus 18, consider these relationally intentional efforts.

First, identify your people. Great leaders have a network of folks both outside and inside their small group who intentionally pour into them, equipping and encouraging them to continue pouring out in their groups.

This network is comprised of those who provide authentic friendship and genuine direction. They are individuals who are "pro you," and who, no matter the circumstance, are ready and willing to walk the extra mile with you while demonstrating truth and love. Here's how you can identify your people, using Moses' father-in-law, Jethro, as a guide:

- Jethro asked Moses tough questions. Who gets to ask you the tough questions that challenge and move you forward?
- Moses trusted Jethro. Who do you trust? Who has access to your heart and the innermost parts of your life?
- Jethro poured into Moses. Who is pouring into you? Who is developing and sharpening you as a leader?

If you struggled to come up with at least one or two people, then it's worthwhile to put some effort into building up your network of support. Consider someone who is just a step outside of your trusted circle. Could that person become more of a trusted friend? Take them to coffee or lunch, and share a story about yourself to see how they respond. There may also be individuals connected to your small groups ministry who can help. Once you've identified your core people, it's helpful to look inward.

Take your pain to your people. Just as sharing your story positively contributes to your group (refer back to chapter 6), embracing the pain and heartache you've experienced and sharing it with your core people may be the path to greater group health and effectiveness as a leader. Reflect with your trusted friends on these questions:

- What experiences have nearly knocked the breath out of you?
- What people or situations make you frustrated or angry?
- What parts of yourself and your life do you not share with others?

Interestingly, organic matter is made up of seemingly ugly components. Compost is really just leftover plant material, and manure is expelled, leftover "waste." But when applied in the right way, they produce life. Identify your pain and take it to your people. Embrace the transformative possibilities that are buried within your pain. Community redeems the brokenness and messiness of life.

YOU MUST CARE FOR YOURSELF

You can have both: care for yourself *and* care for your group. In fact, engaging in spiritual and emotional self-care fuels care for your group. Yes, you can rest and exhale in your leadership without exiting or abdicating your role. As you enjoy God's Word, pray with intimacy, worship with passion, and pursue community intentionally, your spiritual soil may yield much fruit, making deeper and longer-lasting leadership possible.

YOUR SELF-CARE PLAN

Complete the plan below for this week and then start a new one each week, noting progress over time.

	WHERE I AM RIGHT NOW:	WHERE I WANT TO BE:	WHAT I CAN DO THIS WEEK TO MOVE FROM WHERE I AM TO WHERE I WANT TO BE:
Enjoying God's Word	(e.g., Reading the Bible when I have time, randomly picking a passage each time, or reading a few verses each week)	(e.g., Reading and journaling every day, finding a Scripture to claim for myself, working on a Bible study)	(e.g., finding a place, researching HeReadsTruth or SheReadsTruth for a study, or calling a mentor or pastor for recommendations)
Praying with Intimacy	(e.g., praying only at meals and in desperate times)	(e.g., praying for group members regularly, praying the Lord's Prayer, establishing a dedicated prayer time in my schedule)	(e. g., learning the ACTS model for prayer, scheduling ten minutes each day to pray, asking others about their prayer practices)
Worshipping with Passion	(e.g., nonexistent, listening to worship music)	(e.g., reading a Psalm out loud each day, memorizing worship songs filled with Scripture, verbally praising God)	(e.g., asking a friend for a playlist, scheduling a hike alone, intentionally seeking to appreciate God's creation, finding a book on work as worship)
Pursuing Community Intentionally	(e.g., in a small group, have a mentor)	(e.g., identify people, pain, and protections; understand my boundaries; know who will keep me accountable in my leadership responsibilities)	(e.g., set aside an hour to pray through a list of people, begin a list of boundaries to discuss with a trusted friend)

LEAD FROM THE INSIDE OUT

Pete Scazzero

Does any of the following resonate with you?

> You can't shake the pressure you feel from having too much to do in too little time.
> You are always rushing.
> You routinely fire off quick opinions and judgments.
> You are fearful about the future.
> You are overly concerned with what others think.
> You are defensive and easily offended.
> You are constantly preoccupied and distracted.
> You consistently ignore the stress, anxiety, and tightness of your body.
> You feel unenthusiastic or threatened by the success of others.
> You regularly spend more time talking than listening.

If so, you might be what I call an emotionally unhealthy leader, someone who operates in a continuous state of emotional and spiritual deficit, lacking the emotional maturity and a consistent "being with God" that is sufficient to sustain a "doing for God."

Be honest: does that label fit you?

Unhealthy Christian leaders suffer from emotional and spiritual formation deficits that impact every aspect of their lives.

Unhealthy leaders lack self-awareness. Unaware of what is going on inside them, they ignore emotion-related messages their body may send—fatigue, stress-induced

illness, weight gain, ulcers, headaches, or depression—
and avoid reflecting on their fear, sadness, or anger.
Moreover, they're often blind to the emotional impact
they have on others, especially in their leadership role.

**Unhealthy leaders prioritize ministry over marriage or
singleness.** Though these leaders affirm the importance
of a healthy intimacy in relationships and lifestyle, they
don't have a vision for their marriage or singleness as
the greatest gift they offer to the church and the world.
Instead, they view their marriage or singleness as an
essential and stable foundation for something more
important: building an effective ministry.

**Unhealthy leaders do more activity for God than their
relationship with God can sustain.** They're chronically overextended. They say "yes" to too many good
opportunities before prayerfully and carefully discerning God's will. They view time spent in solitude
and silence as a luxury or something best suited for
a different kind of leader, not something essential for
effective leadership.

Unhealthy leaders lack a work-Sabbath rhythm. They
don't practice a Sabbath—a weekly, twenty-four-hour
period in which they cease working to rest, delight in
God's gifts, and enjoy life with him. To them, Sabbath
observance is irrelevant, optional, or even a burden-
some legalism that belongs to an ancient past.

While it's true that none of the characteristics above seem
especially dramatic, these leaders and those they lead eventually
pay a heavy price for such chronically unhealthy behaviors.

But it doesn't have to be that way. The journey to becoming
an emotionally healthy leader can be summarized in ten words:
What you do matters; who you are matters much more.

Emotionally healthy leaders operate with an emotionally and spiritually "full" cup, such that their deep walk with God sustains what they do for God. They make significant and sustainable impact.

I encourage you to take seriously your own health as a small group leader. You can't take your group to places you haven't gone yourself.

While many issues are important to developing and transforming the inner life of a leader, four stand out to me as foundational, both in my own life and in two decades of mentoring other leaders. To lead from a deep and transformed inner life:

Face your "shadow."
Lead out of your marriage or singleness.
Slow down for loving union with God.
Practice Sabbath delight.

Your group members are watching your life to see how you live out your faith. The healthiest leaders are the best followers— those who bring their words, time, energy, and priorities into alignment with Jesus' example. When you make Christ the center of your focus, unhealthy patterns will begin to fall away, and others will "see your good works and give glory to your Father who is in heaven" (Matt. 5:16).

Stay with it, take one step at a time, and neither you nor those you lead will ever be the same.

Peter Scazzero is the founder of New Life Fellowship Church in Queens, New York City and now serves Emotionally Healthy Discipleship. He is the author of a number of bestselling books, including *The Emotionally Healthy Leader* and *Emotionally Healthy Spirituality*. To connect with Pete, visit EmotionallyHealthy.org or connect on Twitter at @petescazzero.

KEY TAKEAWAYS

1. Remember that your group members tend to look to you, as their leader, to model spiritual health.
2. To set yourself up for continued health and impact, take advantage of your protections in the form of training, mentors, and trusted friends.
3. To effectively deal with the many pressures of life and leading groups, remain diligent to not only stay healthy, but to thrive and grow through the ups and downs of small group leadership.
4. Cultivate and nourish your spiritual soil through your discipline and engagement in four key areas: enjoying God's Word, praying with intimacy, worshipping with passion, and pursuing community intentionally.
5. Continually take time and invest energy to nourish your soul and care for yourself. It will be good for you and your group.

REFLECTION AND DISCUSSION QUESTIONS

First, take some time to individually reflect on these questions on leadership burnout:[9]

1. What do I expect others to give me?
2. Who do I hope will affirm me?
3. Who am I trying to please?
4. How honest am I being with myself and others?
5. What lie am I believing?

Second, engage these questions with others:

1. What did God reveal to you through the reflection activity and prompt?
2. **Remember:** What caught your attention in this chapter about care and sustainable leadership?

3. 🦉**Understand:** What is the relationship between your small group leadership and your personal spiritual health habits and behaviors?

4. ⚙**Apply:** Which of the spiritual enrichment habits come(s) most naturally to you?

5. 🔍**Analyze:** Which one(s) might need your intentional pursuit?

6. 📋**Evaluate:** What gets in the way of your pursuit of these organic habits? What does that reveal about your current condition?

7. 💡**Create:** What are your two most concrete action steps related to these organic habits?

CHAPTER 10

YOUR LEGACY

Recruiting and Raising Up New Leaders

*You then, my child, be strengthened by the grace that
is in Christ Jesus, and what you have heard from
me in the presence of many witnesses entrust to
faithful men, who will be able to teach others also.*

—PAUL, 2 TIMOTHY 2:1-2

Leaders don't create followers. They create more leaders.

—TOM PETERS

When you have a family emergency, does your group meet without you? When you've had a long week and feel unprepared for your group meeting, are you confident someone else will step up and carry the load? If your groups pastor asked you to name 2–3 people in your group who could lead a new group, do you have those names on the tip of your tongue?

If you answered "no" to one or more of these questions, this chapter is especially for you. You're probably craving greater leadership capacity for your group members. And there are likely leaders out there who could use your encouragement to step into their call-ing to lead and influence.

Sharing the leadership load will not only make your group more effective, but also reduce the pressure that's placed on your shoul-ders. Sara, a small group leader in the Midwest, experienced this shift in her group: "When we went on vacation early on in the life of our group, our members wouldn't meet. Now, they meet and are fine. They shouldn't be dependent on the leader."

Are you able to say, like Sara, that your group is no longer dependent on you?

Our data shows that both group leaders and pastors are always thinking about training and developing thriving leaders. This isn't surprising. Prioritizing leadership development brings sustained health to group members and will deeply impact the culture of a small groups ministry.

Unfortunately, one reason church and ministry leaders are so intent on developing leaders is that it's not an easy process. In this chapter, we'll explore some common challenges people encounter when attempting to develop leaders and explore three simple, proven strategies you can employ to identify, recruit, and raise up new lead-ers. Not only will you expand your ministry as new leaders carry on the work you began, but you'll also feel great freedom to move into whatever God is calling you to next without unnecessary concern about what will happen to your group without you leading.

FIVE PITFALLS IN DEVELOPING LEADERS

Both pastors and leaders indicated to us that their greatest needs are recruiting and developing leaders. Even though ministries are spending a ton of time and resources discussing strategies to do just that, there still are not enough effective leaders.

If we cannot consistently raise up new leaders, the growth and impact of small groups are stymied.

Certainly we need more leaders, but we also need better, more effective leaders. As we mentioned earlier, when a ministry is able to send out a sufficient number of equipped leaders, incredible movements are made possible.

In our research, two-thirds of groups surveyed indicated that they had sent out at least one person or couple to lead a new group, while only 4.5 percent of the groups surveyed had sent out more than two people or couples. On one hand, that's incredible—two-thirds of the most effective groups we studied have sent out leaders. But that also means almost one-third of the groups pastors identified as effective have not sent out capable leaders to lead new groups.

Why is the church unable to raise a sufficient number of qualified leaders? We believe there are five primary reasons.

TOO MANY LEADERS TRY TO DO TOO MUCH.

One of the greatest culprits of a lack of leadership development is leaders taking on too much. Too many leaders have a "Superman" or "Superwoman" complex. OK, this might get awkward for a moment, but think about it:

- Do you sometimes take on more than your fair share in your relationships?
- Do your perfectionistic tendencies push you to make sure everything in your group is "just right"?
- Does your need to be needed (Ouch! We know this might be painful!) spur you to be more available than you should be?
- Does your competence drive you to keep tasks to yourself because you know you can accomplish them better than others?

In his excellent book *Hero Maker*, Dave Ferguson of Community Christian Church in Illinois explained what happens all too often:

> Way too many times in ministry, I've jumped in with "I've got it!" or even "This is my sweet spot," and it never occurred to me—until too late—that I was blocking other people from the privilege and joy of using *their* faith or serving in *their* sweet spot.[1]

When you take on too much, others don't have the space they need to bring their gifts and talents to the group, and you get more of what you ultimately don't want—more responsibility, more pressure, more ownership.

> When you take on too much, others don't have the space they need to bring their gifts and talents to the group, and you get more of what you ultimately don't want—more responsibility, more pressure, more ownership.

One of the biggest reasons leaders don't step forward is because of *too much* leader activity, not too little. If you want to create space for people to take on greater leadership, perhaps the best thing you can do is to *strategically not do.*

THE FOCUS OF TOO MANY GROUPS IS INSULAR.

Another reason the church experiences a lack of effective leaders is because groups focus too much internally, and not enough externally. When groups are only and always about the people inside the group, there's a tendency to protect and preserve what already exists. This discourages emerging leaders from driving innovation and change, and creatively pursuing and connecting with others outside the group. Great leaders push out the artificial boundaries of the group and influence group members to look and live outward. This requires greater leadership capacity.

THE LEADER ROLE IS TOO SMALL.

There's no need to identify or develop additional leaders when being a leader is super simple. Why bring a team together to make a peanut-butter-and-jelly sandwich? You wouldn't. There's no need. Beyond that, a group trying to make a sandwich would suffer from too many cooks in the kitchen.

When leading a group is as simple as reading a list of questions about Sunday's sermon, there's no need to spread the leadership burden. When groups take on more—often by framing and pursuing a purpose that is bigger than themselves—additional leadership is necessary, and that bigger mission opens up space for new leaders to fill.

LEADERS (AND FOLLOWERS) DON'T CONCEIVE THAT THE LEADERSHIP ROLE IS ABOUT BUILDING OTHER LEADERS.

During his sophomore year of college, Ryan was a resident assistant, a role where a veteran student assists those new to the college experience by building community and serving as a resource. His future wife, Jill, happened to be one of his residents (a bit sketchy, we know, but don't worry—they weren't dating then). A few years later, they were reflecting on Ryan's effectiveness as an RA. Ultimately, they disagreed about what kind of a leader he was. Jill wasn't super impressed by his leadership; she said he wasn't around much and that he didn't engage her and others in their community enough in long, deep conversations. When Ryan asked her if she felt connected to the other members of their community and if she had long, deep conversations with others on campus, she said, "Yes!" without hesitation. Their perceptions of good leadership were quite different. For Jill, in that season and situation, leadership was about what the leader did. And she's certainly not alone in that view. Many people would agree. We don't fully disagree, either. What leaders do is incredibly important. But what they spur on for and in others is even more important.

Again, Dave Ferguson offers a great question to ask: "Am I trying to be the hero, or am I trying to make heroes out of others?"[2] Leadership isn't all about being a hero, but making heroes out of others. For many leaders, that mental model of leadership has to shift.

SYSTEMS DON'T EXIST TO IDENTIFY AND BUILD LEADERS.

Finally, there are not enough effective leaders because the church often lacks systems to identify, develop, and deploy leaders. Leadership development often lives as a "would be nice to do" task item rather than a "the building or program will collapse if we don't" issue. So it remains on the back burner. People with incredible leadership capacity and/or potential sit on the sidelines rather than stepping into the game. We all must build easy and effective on-ramps into small group leadership.

YOUR LEADERSHIP DEVELOPMENT PLAN

As a group leader, you have an incredible opportunity to develop other leaders. Developing and releasing new leaders brings a group's development full circle. There are two important steps within this process. The first step is something we've already covered: it involves raising up group members who participate in owning the group and helping it be all it can be (which we discussed in chapter 6). Once you're seeing shared ownership within the group, it's time to take the next step and focus on developing your leadership-oriented group members so they will be ready to be sent out as new group leaders.

Here's the good news: you don't need to wait for someone to empower you to identify and develop leaders. You can start right now. So here's a three-phase approach to developing leaders and expanding your influence:

YOUR LEADERSHIP DEVELOPMENT PLAN

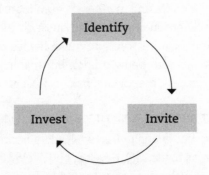

IDENTIFY: WHAT ARE YOU LOOKING FOR?

Small groups pastors identified three key requirements for becoming a leader:

1. The potential leader must be currently participating in a group (76 percent said this was somewhat to very important).
2. They should be nominated by an existing small group or church leader (68 percent said this was somewhat to very important).
3. The potential leader must have completed the church's assimilation process (61 percent said this was somewhat to very important).

By comparison, only 52 percent of pastors reported that individuals taking a leadership training course was a requirement, while 41 percent of pastors identified current engagement in a discipleship relationship as a requirement.

REQUIREMENTS FOR LEADERSHIP ACCORDING TO PASTORS

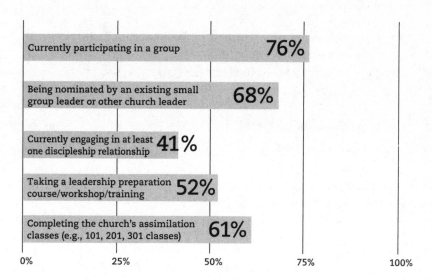

In order to raise up additional leaders, you need to intentionally identify and recommend people in your group who could serve as leaders. However, the vast majority of group leaders are not raising up leaders-in-training. Less than 10 percent of pastors report that more than half of their leaders are raising up leaders, as indicated in the graph above.

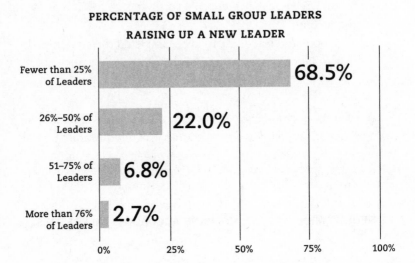

PERCENTAGE OF SMALL GROUP LEADERS RAISING UP A NEW LEADER

We want to remove as many roadblocks as possible so you can begin to raise up leaders and increase your influence.

Here's how you identify the right people.

Look for the usual suspects.

Pastors identified these top five qualifications for small group leaders:

1. Personal integrity
2. Teachability
3. Personal spiritual maturity
4. Availability
5. Transparency

That's a pretty solid list that focuses in on character and who people are. As you think about your group members, who exhibits these traits?

Perhaps you prefer to take your cues from leaders of the most effective groups we studied. When small group leader Linda looks for potential leaders, she looks for members who deeply participate in discussions, looking for key life applications; build relationships with others in the group and outside the group; and are willing to honestly speak about their struggles. She looks for people who are deeply engaged in the group and are already leaning into their own growth and contributing to the growth of others. Small group leader Jean looks for a willingness to serve, a depth in understanding the group's discussion content, a willingness to vocalize thoughts, and a commitment to care for other group members.

Notice natural gatherers.

Particularly when considering starting a brand-new group or continuing on with a group that has benefitted from leaders who were effective at pulling the group together, look for people with demonstrated gathering ability. You know a natural gatherer when you see one; they're the people other people flock to or gravitate toward. You can see people respond positively to their invitation to connect. Small group leader Alina noticed one particular member who connected well with everyone in the group. He was planning activities outside of group, he attended consistently, and he participated regularly in discussions. The fruits of the Spirit were evident in him. He was a natural gatherer and a great candidate for taking on greater leadership.

Especially when a group is first coming together, the group members' needs for safety and connection are nicely addressed by people who know how to gather and connect with other people. Without overplaying any single quality, and knowing that a combination of the top qualities is best, think both inside and outside of your small group: Who around you is a natural gatherer?

Consider people outside your group.

There are some folks who would be great group leaders who are not in your group. In fact, 13 percent of the group leaders we surveyed indicated they led a group without having any other previous group experience. Who do you know who is not currently plugged into a group but exhibits the characteristics noted above?

Be careful when the wrong person seeks leadership.

Before we talk about inviting people into greater leadership, we should address the awkward situation that arises when people who really want to be leaders don't exhibit the traits above. We encourage you to do the following with these folks:

1. Have an honest conversation with them. Affirm their desire. The desire to lead is a noble one. Kindly, graciously, and honestly share with them what you see. "Mariah, I see that you go the extra mile to make other group members feel comfortable, but I don't see you regularly contributing to our discussions about the book we're reading. Can we talk more about that?"
2. Work with them to help them grow in areas of insecurity and weakness.
3. Give them small roles in which they can demonstrate leadership, and coach them as they do.

Your willingness to engage a loving but candid conversation just might be the nudge they need to take their own growth seriously and devote time and attention to it.

TWO-MINUTE TIP

Name 2–3 people who come to mind when you think of developing new leaders. Next to their names, write down what you see in them that reflects their leadership ability or potential.

INVITE: HOW CAN YOU GIVE POTENTIAL LEADERS OPPORTUNITY?

There's great power in being asked. This is what Jesus did with the disciples—and it's what you can do with others. Here's how to do it well:

Affirm giftings you see in others.

As small group leader Ike shared, when you edify others, it often begins the process of raising up new leaders. He shared that there wasn't a particular moment, but rather many small discussions over weeks and months affirming one couple's gift of hospitality. "Generally, when I edify their gifts, they usually come back and kind of pitch the idea of taking something on. And I'll ask, 'What could that look like for you?' which often includes them telling me about their timing, their fears, and other things they've been thinking about."

> There's great power in being asked. This is what Jesus did with the disciples—and it's what you can do with others.

Consider inviting someone to lunch or coffee, then sharing what you see in them and your vision for their next step in leadership. There's something special about being called out and told what someone sees in you—at least when it is positive. Take the time and energy to affirm others' giftings and strengths to start the process of inviting.

Invite potential leaders to try out leadership in your group.

Ask them to try leading the prayer time or facilitating a sermon discussion or organizing the meal plan. Help them understand that leadership isn't a title, but an action. Then, allow them room for error and growth as they test their wings. One of the easiest ways to do this is by not doing. In fact, resist the urge to be a "perfect" leader.

Allow the food preparations to be less-than-ideal, let the conversation awkwardly stall, and wait for others to step forward. In essence, be strategically incompetent, as it will create space and structure for a potential leader to empower her/himself.

Invite potential leaders to help you develop a compelling direction for your group.

As discussed in chapter 4, involving others in clarifying the direction of your group can reap huge rewards, as it creates buy-in and ownership. Ask potential leaders to chime in on what your group needs and what it should do next.

Recognize your limitations, and invite potential leaders to help the group overcome them.

First, you may need to swallow a humility pill. If you think you're better at most things than others (be honest with yourself), realize that's likely not true. There are other people who can do things far better than you. Second, grounded in that humility, ask your apprentices to see your weaknesses and then identify how they can help mitigate those challenges. Maybe you could use help in inviting more people to the group, cultivating rich discussions, or reining in the negative influence of certain group members. Ask for help. The group will be better off, and you'll feel less pressure to succeed even in your weak spots.

Want leadership for your apprentices, not just from them.

No matter what strategies you use to invite members into leadership, make sure your heart is in the right place. Recruiting and raising up new leaders isn't about you or reducing your workload. Instead, it's about recognizing and equipping potential leaders to step further into their unique callings, expand their influence, and be used to extend God's kingdom. In short, want leadership *for* them, not just *from* them.

INVEST: HOW CAN YOU POUR INTO EMERGING LEADERS?

Once you've identified and invited some potential candidates to engage and develop, your next step is to intentionally invest in them. Here are some ideas:

Invest individually as a mentor and/or discipler.

You have an incredible opportunity to pour yourself into your group members. Less than 50 percent of group members report being actively discipled. Imagine the potential for spiritual growth and development that could occur if you poured your life into a few people.

Bring your potential leaders with you.

Most churches offer continuing development opportunities for their leaders—bring your potential leaders with you and get them signed up for email and video leadership development. This serves several goals. First, it serves an acculturation function by helping these future leaders learn what group leadership entails. Second, as they learn what leadership looks like, they can step into areas where they can help you, and in some cases, they will do it better than you do. Finally, this begins their leadership development journey before they are leading, giving them a head start on cultivating the necessary skills they'll need to lead an effective group.

Draw emerging leaders into leadership functions in your group.

Consider what new leaders can take on, then give it to them, and coach along the way. The five steps laid out by Dave Ferguson and Warren Bird in *Hero Maker* offer a fantastic guide to help what they call an "apprentice leader" progress from observing to helping to owning more and more leadership in the group.[3]

1. I do. You watch. We talk.

Apprentice leaders pay attention to how the leader leads, then they get together to debrief. They consider what worked and what didn't work, and how can they make group meetings better.

2. I do. You help. We talk.

The apprentice leads particular tasks, such as prayer time or an icebreaker. Then the apprentice gets together with the leader to debrief. The leader can ask the same kinds of questions as before, but also ask how the apprentice felt taking that step of leadership.

3. You do. I help. We talk.

At this point, the apprentice's portion of leadership crosses the 50 percent threshold, and he or she takes on more than the initial leader. Often, savvy leaders present these opportunities for greater engagement as necessities, because the original leader is too busy with other projects or a busy season of life. Sneaky, we know. Since the apprentice has seen it done many times before, he's ready for the additional leadership. Once again, the apprentice and leader debrief and talk about where the apprentice excelled and how he or she can continually improve.

4. You do. I watch. We talk.

The temptation here for the original leader is to take off and leave the group in the hands of the new leader. Resist that urge. The apprentice leads, the mentor observes and coaches. Then, they talk about whether the apprentice wants to take over the current group or start a new one, and what the original leader will now do.

5. You do. Someone else watches.

Finally, the process of leadership development comes full circle. The apprentice now seeks an apprentice for themselves, and the process repeats itself. The mentor continues to coach and support, and raises up additional apprentices.

Shift your focus from doing the ministry to equipping others to do it.

Rather than actually building the fire, focus your efforts on gathering the kindling necessary for others to build and start a fire. Set the stage for your apprentices to lead effectively.

Share what you are doing with others.

Inform the other members of your group, as well as your ministry coach and pastor, what you are doing and why. Doing so puts those rising leaders on their radar and helps clear the path for their leadership in the future. That's it. IDENTIFY → INVITE → INVEST.

Chad has been leading small groups for almost ten years. Whenever he starts a new group or is in a new season, he strategically looks for new leaders. Within the first three gatherings of a new or reforming group, Chad identifies one or two potential leaders. Then, he invites them out for a one-on-one coffee or lunch. His only agenda at this meeting is to inspire the potential leader by talking about one or two things he sees in them and encouraging them to keep doing those things. As the semester continues, Chad gradually invites that person to take on more responsibility, then invites them out to coffee or lunch again to talk through those leadership experiences. Chad's investments have so far produced leaders for four new small groups.

TWO-MINUTE TIP

Go back to each of the three headings: Identify, Invite, Invest. Circle the stage(s) you've already completed. For the remaining steps (or all three of them!), put tentative deadlines on your calendar for moving forward and put those plans on your to-do list.

Taking those three steps will enable you to avoid the pitfalls of leadership development—and help you begin to expand and sustain the influence you have as a leader.

FOR THE POTENTIAL LEADERS

Maybe you've read this book with a great desire to be an influential leader, but you haven't yet been tapped on the shoulder. And you've been patiently (or not-so-patiently!) waiting. We want to encourage you and offer you a few tips.

Be a really good group member. Great leaders are great members. Do what your leader asks you to do with excellence and precision. This is a good time to apply the truth of Ecclesiastes 9:10: "Whatever your hand finds to do, do it with your might." Ultimately, there's a small gap between what good group members do and what group leaders do. Good group members often end up leading a group.

Start leading. Don't wait for your formal leader to recognize you or to ask. Here's the question to ask: *What does my group need right now?* Identify that, then provide it. If it is encouragement, then encourage people. If it is more authenticity, then open up and share your life with vulnerability. If it is logistics, then help organize the meal schedule or an upcoming service project. If it is a greater purpose, then be willing to initiate the conversation, and invite your group to join you in the activities you are doing to be missional in your neighborhood or community. Don't wait for someone to tap you with the empowerment wand; just start.

Ask God to make you visible to your group leader and to your church/ministry leadership. Resist the urge to make yourself known. Let God shine his light on you and give you favor with your formal leaders.

Start small and look around you. If you're not currently in a group, why not start your own group? Ask a group of people around you if they'd like to meet and do life together. Apply the tips we've shared in chapters 4 and 5 to successfully gather your group and launch it. The key here is not to overthink or to overanalyze. Take the initiative and get going.

Jesus' parable of the talents, recounted in Matthew 25, tells the story of three servants who were given various amounts of "talents." After a period of time, the master came back and inspected what those servants did with those talents. The servants who multiplied their talents were rewarded, while the one who hid his talent was punished. Here's what the master said to the two servants who used and cultivated their talents: "Well done, good and faithful servant. You have been faithful over a little; I will set you over much" (Matt. 25:21).

Let us repeat that: "You have been faithful over a little; I will set you over much." Take the initiative, start small, and see what God sets you over as you surrender yourself to him and cultivate your skills to lead effectively.

THE POWER OF ENOUGH EQUIPPED LEADERS

What would happen if an army of equipped leaders arose in your church, your ministry, your movement, your community? Scores of people would enjoy relational connection and grow more fully into the people God designed them to be.

Every one of you gets to participate in raising up those leaders. Sure, start small. But start somewhere. And then watch how God increases your influence and expands your impact far beyond what you can do yourself.

GUEST COMMENTARY

TAPPING INTO THE LEADERSHIP POTENTIAL OF THE MAJORITY OF YOUR CONGREGATION

Kadi Cole

"Oh, I could never *lead* the group." Isabella burst into laughter, as if this was the craziest thing her pastor had ever suggested.

"But, Isabella," he explained, "you *already* lead the group in many ways. You arrive early to greet everyone and make them feel welcome. You text and talk with people throughout the week. You encourage them and pray for them. You have great things to say during our discussions. In fact, our last two guests came because you invited them!" Isabella wasn't convinced. She turned down the opportunity to lead, leaving her pastor confused.

I hear stories like this all the time. Pastors and group leaders identify faithful, gifted, capable female leaders. The problem is, these women not only resist stepping into leadership, but often have a hard time even *thinking* of themselves as leaders! Could we be missing something?

Although women make up 61 percent of most church congregations, they hold less than 10 percent of formal leadership roles (this includes small group leaders). Depending on your church's theology, there may be boundaries around the kinds of groups women can lead or the roles they can fill. However, my research shows that churches across the theological spectrum are greatly underutilizing the leadership capacity of the women in their congregations—often without realizing it.

How can we change this?

First, we must be aware of the *sticky floor*.

You've probably heard of the "glass ceiling." It's made up of unseen organizational barriers that keep women from progressing in leadership. Your church may have a glass ceiling of sorts; but more important for group leaders to be aware of is the sticky floor: the internal dialogues and assumptions women have *about themselves* that hold them back from accepting opportunities to grow and advance as leaders. One research project reveals that when a man looks at a leadership opportunity (such as applying to be a small group leader), he tends to review the job description from a positive perspective. As long as he feels confident that he can perform 60 percent of the position requirements, he will apply. Men are generally confident that they can "figure it out" as they go. A woman, on the other hand, will look at the same job description and, unless she feels 100 percent confident of her ability to perform every item on the list, *will not even apply*.

This reality has huge implications for us as we recruit female leaders. Because men and women look at opportunities differently, we need to adapt our practices as we invite and invest in female leaders. When we talk with a future female leader, we must help her see that she is a strong candidate for the role.

In fact, it is likely she's already fulfilling the responsibilities. Explain that you will train her, and that you know it might take a few months for her to grow into the full scope of her responsibilities. Cast a vision for why you think God may be calling her to this role, and help her rest in his grace—reassure her that she doesn't have to be perfect, that you believe in her abilities and God's call on her life. Help her begin to see herself the way you and God already see her: as a leader.

Second, we must be aware of our own biases.

We all have biases and preferences; it's part of what makes us human. However, our biases and preferences can stand in the way of the kingdom when we use them as an excuse to *not* include all those God has gifted to lead.

The topic of women in leadership is long-debated and emotionally charged. However, leaders are beginning to realize that the biases and limitations they mentally place on women are often less about their own theology and more about the culture in which they grew up.[4]

Challenge yourself to learn more about how your biases affect your leadership. Do you have a habit of offering opportunities to women only when it comes to gender-based roles, such as food preparation, childcare, or delivering meals? Do you give specific, constructive feedback to men on how they can improve but shy away from doing the same for the women you lead? Most women only receive "vague praise," without enough specifics to actually develop their skills, while men often receive clear, consistent feedback. Do you tend to "check in" with, or even "get permission" from a woman's husband before offering her an opportunity to serve or lead?

In my research, I have found that both men and women alike have unconscious biases. These stereotypes greatly limit the potential of those we lead. However, when we begin to look critically at our habits and inherited mindsets with fresh eyes, we can start to shift our personal leadership practices to be more inclusive not only of women, but of *all the richly diverse people* God has brought into our sphere of influence. Only then can we fully release the leadership potential of our whole church.

———————————

Kadi Cole is a leadership consultant and bestselling author of *Developing Female Leaders: Navigate the Minefields and Release the Potential of Women in Your Church*. Learn more at KadiCole.com or connect with her @kadicole.

KEY TAKEAWAYS

1. Don't take on too much as a leader. When you do, you discourage others from stepping into leadership and fulfilling that call on their own lives.
2. Use your leadership position to identify, invite, and invest in new leaders.
3. When searching for potential leaders, look for natural gatherers, and for people who demonstrate personal integrity, teachability, and spiritual maturity. Don't forget to look outside your group for these people, too.
4. To invite potential leaders to consider taking on more leadership, affirm their giftings and give them chances to try out leadership in a variety of different ways.
5. Invest in emerging leaders by mentoring or discipling them, bringing them to leadership development events, and gradually turning over more leadership duties to them.

REFLECTION AND DISCUSSION QUESTIONS

1. 👆**Remember:** What caught your attention in this chapter about developing leaders?

2. 🦉**Understand:** Which element of the three-phase leadership development plan is most important? Which one is most neglected?
3. ⚙️**Apply:** At which of the three phases do you need to start?
4. 🔍**Analyze:** From that starting point, what potential do you see in moving forward in leadership development within your specific small group?
5. 📋**Evaluate:** What could hinder your leadership development efforts? How might you overcome those challenges?
6. 💡**Create:** Outline a plan for raising up a new small group leader in the next season of group life.

CHAPTER 11

YOUR CHARGE

Expanding and Multiplying Groups

Be fruitful and multiply.

—GOD, GENESIS 1:28

The church is like manure.
Pile it together and it stinks up the neighborhood;
spread it out and it enriches the world.

—LUIS PALAU

It's time for an apology. Through the first ten chapters of this book, we've led you to believe that a thriving small group is the end goal. We've shared research and stories to give you guidance on how you can lead thriving small groups. We've shared Two-minute Tips to get you thinking about how to apply this knowledge and expertise to your specific small group. But to be honest, helping you build a thriving small group was only *part* of our aim.

Here's the thing. By now we hope you agree with us that spiritual growth is the desired outcome. That's at least partially achieved through your leading a thriving small group. But, leaders don't just create followers; leaders create new leaders.[1] And biblically, we see that disciples make disciples.

Matthew 28, oftentimes referred to as the Great Commission, says,

> Jesus came and said to [the eleven disciples], "All authority in heaven and on earth has been given to me. Go therefore and make disciples of all nations" (vv. 18–19).

Go and make disciples.

Disciples make disciples. And great small group leaders cultivate more small group leaders who help facilitate spiritual growth in others.

While many of you will agree with that goal, the reality is that we all tend to enjoy comfort. Great groups want to stick together for a long time. Who wants to build a thriving group and then leave it or send out your group members to start a new one? Each of us has been there.

This is *multiplication: to increase through repeated addition.* In other words, disciples make disciples who make disciples. That's what this chapter is about.

IT'S TIME TO THINK ABOUT MULTIPLICATION

From Genesis to Revelation, we see multiplication as God's primary way of spreading the gospel and making disciples. In Genesis 1, God commands Adam and Eve to be fruitful and multiply. This command was not just about having babies. It was more about multiplying the image of God. In Genesis 9, after God floods the earth in response to man's rebellion, Noah and his sons are told to "be fruitful and multiply and fill the earth" (Gen. 1:28). As we reminded you earlier in this chapter, the Great Commission is ultimately about multiplication.

Gospel-centered multiplication is the responsibility of every Christian, not just pastoral staff. And when we say, "gospel-centered," we mean multiplication for the sake of the gospel and the building of God's kingdom, rather than for our own legacy, glory, or kingdom-building.

Not only does multiplication spur more groups wherein people can grow, but it also strengthens the groups that prepare for and engage multiplication. Our data was beautifully clear here: groups that had multiplied were healthier than groups that had not yet multiplied. This has at least four important implications.

Multiplication is one sign of a spiritually healthy group. While it may be tempting to keep adding members to your group, you know from chapters 6 and 7 that this is not necessarily the best idea. Rather, as your group thrives and new members join, consider multiplying.

Spiritual health precedes multiplication, not the other way around. In other words, multiplying a stagnant group won't necessarily contribute to members' spiritual growth. So it's important to focus on cultivating a thriving small group that contributes to individuals' spiritual growth. Then, consider multiplying.

The most effective groups in our study were newer groups. Groups that had been meeting for a shorter amount of time contributed *more* to their members' spiritual growth than groups that had been together longer. (Well, there's one caveat—groups that had been together for eleven or more years actually reported the greatest effectiveness, but they're rare.)

Groups that have multiplied tend to contribute to individuals' spiritual health more than groups that haven't multiplied. When groups first get together, they see a lot of growth early on. But over time, the group becomes more maintenance-oriented than growth-oriented. The group begins to rest on its laurels, its community, how it feels to be in and part of the group, and neglects to continue to pursue its purpose. The group members have realized their desire to be known, and they no longer feel the need to expend effort and energy to keep growing together.

This happens in nearly every kind of community. Take sports franchises, for instance. Who wants to break up groups of people who love to play together? Nobody does, but good general managers know that they must sacrifice comfort for growth. It's the same with personal training. Do the same thing over and over, and your muscles will get used to those movements and no longer grow. But add variety to your workout regimen, and you'll begin to see advances.

This might be as simple as adding a new group member or two. Just like when an all-star joins a team via free agency, even the addition or substitution of one player creates entirely new dynamics.

But what about the community you've cultivated and the investment you've made in these people? Won't multiplication ruin a good thing?

Potentially. But maybe it's a good thing to ruin a good thing. Don't settle for good when you can achieve better.

YOUR GROUP MIGHT NEED INTERVENTION AND/OR INNOVATION

Your group members start showing up ten minutes late, derail conversations away from the topic at hand in favor of more superficial topics, and settle into similar strains of prayer requests. What used to be lively and challenging is now banal and dull. Sound familiar?

This is the tendency of almost every group over time. Previously effective groups grow comfortable. Without intervention or innovation, these groups slowly become less effective. This is not surprising. Systemic approaches to groups and organizations suggest that most groups and organizations decline in quality and decay over time unless change is introduced to those systems.

As a result, the continual spurring on toward love and good deeds (see Hebrews 10) in groups grows increasingly challenging as time progresses. To ward off the natural decay of groups, multiplication is a necessary intervention and innovation.

Without direct interventions such as adding new group members, sharing leadership, or redefining your purpose, the group will decay. Take yourself as an example. Without proper feeding, exercise, and medicinal interventions, your body will run down much sooner than you'd like.

Likewise, your group cannot keep doing the same thing over and over and expect different results. We know what that behavior produces. You wouldn't do the same workout day after day, year after year if you are hoping to be physically fit. Innovative approaches to your group (and your health) unlock new life, vitality, and growth. The same must be true for your group to continue to thrive. Sometimes group activities, such as prayer walking, evangelism, serving and ministering to other people, and worshipping in your group gatherings, can reinvigorate your group experience.

At other times, a greater change is necessary, such as a change of leadership, a change of people gathering together, or a change of scenery. Multiplication might be the change needed to yield better groups.

GROUP MULTIPLICATION AS BOTH INNOVATION AND INTERVENTION

Multiplication has the potential to yield more groups, and by extension, more good. But in order to cultivate more good, groups must fight against the idol of comfort. Many of us want to get to the point where we're leading a thriving group. That's not inherently a bad thing. But we make a *good* thing an *ultimate* thing when we're not willing to give it up for the sake of the gospel. If you're leading a thriving group, consider how many *more* people could grow spiritually by being in a group with at least some of your people. We understand the great temptation and desire to continue to enjoy the community you've worked hard to cultivate, yet you and your group members must be willing to sacrifice your lives for the sake of the gospel. That might mean sacrificing the comfort of your small group environment. We understand that "breaking up is hard to do." One of the primary reasons that the "breakup" talk is so jarring is because romantic relationships are supposed to continue on indefinitely, and breaking up is a sign of a bad thing. But in the context of kingdom multiplication, "breaking up" groups is a sign of progress, growth, and missional focus.

Better groups are possible because of change and innovation.

Your next best move for the sake of the gospel may be to invite new voices into the conversation. Maybe you need to invite some new folks into your group. Sure, it will shake the group dynamic, but quite possibly in a positive direction. More good can be done as you invite new voices into conversations and send others out to lead people into growing relationships with Jesus Christ.

Don't elevate a "good group" over the spreading of the gospel and the growth of God's people. As it has been said, the enemy of the best is the good enough. Don't settle.

CAREFULLY CONSIDER WHEN TO MULTIPLY

So when should you multiply? Not today.

Now that you've breathed that sigh of relief, you're probably wondering at what point you should *think* about multiplying. The answer is that you should think *regularly* about multiplying *regularly*. Multiplication is not something you think and talk about once you get to a particular stage in your group. Rather, groups should talk about continually growing and multiplying in their initial conversations about purpose. Make multiplication part of the DNA of your group—constantly consider and talk about how your group can grow, expand, and increase its impact. These ongoing conversations will normalize change and growth and help your group avoid the anxiety and displacement that comes when the "breakup" talk suddenly is thrown into a group's discourse.

That doesn't mean you should multiply too quickly. Our study showed that 50 percent of all multiplying groups take twenty months or more to do so. They had invested a significant amount of time together, and then decided to multiply their impact.

Consider these four questions to determine if your group is ready to multiply.

1. HAVE YOU ACHIEVED YOUR PURPOSE?

Establishing purpose is essential to cultivating thriving small groups. But it's possible that some group purposes might be fulfilled after a season or two. For example, perhaps you're in a young marrieds group whose purpose is to meet couples in the early months and years of their marriages to set their marriages on solid biblical foundations before they start families. Two years into the group, you start noticing that some group members have begun families and are communicating new needs in the group. It's likely time to change things up.

2. ARE YOU GROWING IN NUMBER?

The larger the group, the less individual group members are able to participate. It's simple math. As mentioned in chapter 5, the best groups are smaller in number, and the quality of groups generally decreases with the increase of group members. If your group is regularly experiencing attendance of more than nine core members, consider multiplying.

3. ARE NEW LEADERS READY?

If the answer is no, then this is a great opportunity to begin to identify a few group members in whose leadership potential you would like to invest. Remember, most small group leaders are willing rather than qualified. Check out chapter 10 again for how to do this well.

4. WHAT IS GOD SAYING TO YOU?

Previous small group research has indicated that leaders who spend ninety minutes or more in daily devotions (yes, we know that's a lot of time!) multiplied their groups twice as much as those who spent less than half an hour in devotions.[2] The implications are clear: the more time you spend with God and his Word, the more likely you are to lead a group that expands and engages for the sake of the gospel. Spend time asking God what he wants for you and your group.

MULTIPLY STRATEGICALLY WHEN IT'S TIME

There are many models for multiplying small groups. If your small group is affiliated with a church or ministry, we suggest you consult with your ministry leaders to determine the right next steps toward multiplying your small group. Here, we identify a few ways to do it:

SEND OUT A LEADER WITH A FEW OTHER FOLKS.

This multiplication method resembles gospel-centered church planting in which a small subset of the group steps out together to cultivate a new community of believers. Perhaps you identify a new group leader early on and share with the group the vision for sending her out to start a new group. Spend time investing in her leadership, giving her opportunities to lead the group during a few of your gatherings, praying for her leadership and the group members who God will place in her group, and inviting her into some of the challenges you have experienced. Then, at the appropriate time, send the new leader out with a few other group members and a charge to develop the group's purpose, establish new norms, and cultivate membership.

START A NEW GROUP YOURSELF

This method presupposes you've raised up other leaders within your current group to keep that group going. If you've done that, you and a few group members can start a new group. This method will take time, both to prepare your current group for transition and prepare you and your team to launch. This method also requires you to identify how you will start a new group. Will you organically invite unconnected people you know? Will you utilize ministry on-ramps like a group launch or a connections event to start a new group?

As you consider sending out a leader to start a new group, or starting one yourself, consider your group's circles of influence:

- Who is unconnected in your workplace?
- Who is unconnected in your neighborhood?
- Who is unconnected from your kids' sports teams or other extracurricular activities and clubs?
- Who is unconnected in your extended family?

A simple invite might be all it takes for the next iteration of your small group to form.

> ### TWO-MINUTE TIP
>
> As you invite your group members into the conversation about multiplication, bring a blank poster board to a group gathering and brainstorm together the circles of influence mentioned above. Visually depicting the plentiful harvest will encourage your group members to invite others and add some accountability. Identify a date by which group members may invite others, and on that date, schedule time during your group gathering to share progress reports.

SPLIT YOUR GROUP

This multiplication method takes one group and splits it into two or three groups. This is a great method if you have identified subgroups within the group. Perhaps the young married group now has a few couples with children who would like to move into a more family-centric group with childcare. So a leader for the new young married group makes room for other young married couples, and young families either join another family group or start a new one, inviting new young families into it. Or perhaps you, as the group leader, sense some specific missional purpose among some of the group members, but not others. Help some of them articulate that purpose, and then lay out the two new groups, giving each member an opportunity to see purpose and get on board!

END THE GROUP

This multiplication method entails ending the group, allowing the group members to then scatter into other groups, start new ones, or some combination of the two. Maybe there's a stirring to start afresh on a multitude of fronts. Or maybe you sense from the Holy Spirit that you are to step away from leading in this capacity. Regardless of the direction, you should discuss intentional next steps that help you and your group members multiply their influence with new people and follow up to ensure they've landed somewhere.

> ### TWO-MINUTE TIP
>
> Send an email to a trusted mentor or ministry leader at your church or organization asking them which of the above-mentioned multiplication methods the organization has implemented successfully. This will start the conversation about how to move forward, helping you learn your organization's history of multiplication and the resources available to you.

WHATEVER YOU DO, FINISH WELL

We're big believers that how you end will impact how your group members begin (and to some degree *if* your group members lead or join another group). Keeping in mind that every new group welcomes all the baggage each group member has from a previous small group experience—every spiritual fruit and every instance of brokenness— you have every incentive to finish well.

When it comes time to end your group, there are several steps you can take to enjoy a powerful ending.

HAVE MULTIPLE CONVERSATIONS

This is not a "one and done" conversation. There's nothing more jarring than showing up to your group gathering on a particular evening and finding out all at once that (1) your group is ending, (2) a new leader has been designated, and (3) you have to choose which group you'll join. Don't hit them all at once. No one wants to relive their high school breakup talks!

Instead, have multiple conversations, and invite your group members to participate in the process. This is not supposed to be something that is done to them, but rather something in which they play an active role. Engage at least these three key conversations with your group members:

Raise the Topic

As soon as you understand that multiplication is part of your leadership vision, share that with your group members. You don't need to have identified a new leader or know which of the above-mentioned multiplication models you'll pursue. You don't even really need a plan yet, but introducing the concept and what you understand about the role of multiplication in groups and the spreading of the gospel will help group members start to pray with you and find their role in that process. Perhaps this is one of your first group gatherings and you lay it out alongside the development of your group purpose. Or maybe you've been meeting together and are starting to feel like your group is plateauing, so you raise the topic for conversation.

Share the Vision

When you've identified the person who will step into greater leadership and have a plan for how multiplication will take place for your specific group at this specific time, both new and old leaders can share the vision and purpose of the multiplication plan and then invite group members to participate in deciding how that will take place.

Here's what that conversation could look like: "As you know, we've been talking about and praying through a multiplication plan this small group season, and we have some updates. You all have probably recognized that Angela has been taking on more responsibilities and leadership here in the past couple of weeks so it should not be a big surprise that Angela is now ready and willing to lead a group of her own. Now, we know that this might be tough to step out of this comfortable place, and it might prompt many questions for you about how this might happen."

Your job here as one of the "old" leaders is to focus on the fundamental issues related to change, while allowing group members creative freedom to explore various possibilities. Both the new and old leaders should look for areas of confusion and unforeseen circumstances. Here are some questions for discussion:

- **What do you hope the new group might be like?** Invite one of the new leaders to share a bit about his or her vision and purpose for the new group, and then invite others to contribute what they might like to see as a new group forms.
- **What do you hope both groups retain as we move forward?** This can be an encouraging part of the discussion for everyone as both sets of leaders commit to retaining what has been working well. This may provide a sense of security for all group members involved.
- **When do you think we should end our current season of group gatherings?** Setting an end date helps group members articulate how they're processing the impending change and allows each person to forecast how long they'll need to process and/or make some decisions. Then, maybe they'll collectively decide to wait until summer arrives or some meaningful date in the life of your small group, like after celebrating your fifth year as a group.

Discuss the Plan

A week or two later, present what you know about how the multiplication plan will unfold. Perhaps this includes some of what was previously discussed: a set end date for the current group, the vision and purpose of both groups moving forward, what will be retained from the current group. Invite questions and comments from group members in order to collectively share ownership of this decision.

CELEBRATE WILDLY, AND COMMISSION NEW LEADERS AND GROUPS

When the end date comes, celebrate! Celebrate what the Lord has done in and through your group. Invite group members to come prepared to share what the Lord has done in their lives during the time your group has been gathering together and celebrate his mighty works. When groups do this, group members experience a sense of closure and accomplishment, which is a wonderful way to end the group.

Additionally, commission the leader(s) for their new leadership roles. Invite group members to speak words of encouragement to them and pray together for the next season. If applicable, also commission the group members who will receive newcomers in the next group. This may be everyone! While some may be staying behind and others may be going, pray for each one to continue to participate fully in the discipleship of one another through group gatherings. Pray for the newcomers whose names you might not yet know and for the hospitality of the current group members.

Then eat together. Maybe prepare a special meal or have a potluck feast. Have cake, cookies, and ice cream. When we say celebrate, we mean go big!

GATHER AGAIN INFORMALLY

A few weeks or months into the new group, gather again. Maybe it's a pool party or a meet-up at a park. Invite everyone, newcomers and old group members alike. Maybe it's Friendsgiving or a Saturday game night. Help newcomers put faces to names and share in the fruit of multiplication. Invite people to share how their new groups are going, what they're experiencing, and once again celebrate the work of the Lord in the lives of these people.

JUST THINK ABOUT IT!

Constantly thinking about and intentionally preparing your group for multiplication makes sense and aligns with the gospel message for everyone within your group. But remember, according to our research, only 50 percent of group leaders have actually multiplied their groups in some fashion. Our desired behavior and current behavior are working against each other. If the church is to have thriving, healthy, spiritually growing small groups, then you must seriously consider *how* you will multiply, not *if* you will. Sit on these words by discipler and evangelist Bob McNabb for a moment:

> There is little chance that any church or small group will develop a disciple-making culture if spiritual multiplication is not central in the vision of the leaders and frequently on their lips.[3]

If you have not incorporated multiplication as part of your overall group's purpose, then we encourage you to start that journey. You can intentionally raise up leaders and prepare your group for its next iteration, and you can do it well, but you must first understand that multiplication is an integral part of your group's purpose.

GUEST COMMENTARY

SMALL GROUPS ARE STILL THE ANSWER

Obe Arellano

"Everything I learned about church planting I learned from small groups." That's what my fellow pastors and I used to say at Community Christian Church in the Chicagoland area, where I pastored for eight years. For years, I've loved reproducing and multiplying small groups. Now I'm taking what I've learned to plant a church in Mexico City.

You probably are not a church planter and may think that this phrase does not apply to you. But if you are part of a church that has a small groups ministry or is moving towards starting a small groups ministry, this phrase really does apply to you. Small groups are a perfect ministry that can benefit all aspects of the local church by identifying, developing, and sending new leaders into the community.

Small groups are a leadership incubator. Most of us know several people who have the potential to grow God's kingdom beyond what we could ask or imagine. What would happen if we invested in them, equipped them, challenged them, and nurtured them into new leaders of small groups, ministries, and/or initiatives? All of these things can be accomplished through the power of a small group.

Over the last ten years, I have been a part of churches with healthy and reproducing small groups ministries and have seen how this benefits current leaders, new leaders, and the church as a whole. Small groups have proved to be a safe place where church members can experience community and invite their friends into a nonthreatening environment as a first step towards finding their way back to God. But I have also been a part of churches where small groups are nonexistent. Before planting a church with Community Christian Church in the Chicagoland area, I was a part of a Hispanic church that focused more on having midweek services. Yes, I said *services*. Three, to be exact. And as leader, I had to be in all of them. In fact, everyone who was a member of the church was expected to be at all midweek services.

That's the reality of the majority of Hispanic churches in the United States and churches in Latin America. And all of these churches face the same challenge of midweek services: church fatigue. Sadly, very few are willing to take the risk and make the changes necessary for this important shift. The good news is that there is a small, growing percentage of Hispanic churches that are making the effort to shift from midweek services to a small groups ministry in order to connect their church members in a small community setting during the week. Recently, I coached a church staff in Mexico City that was canceling its midweek service in order to start small groups. After training them to move forward in this initiative, the pastor told me how he could see his church having a greater impact on its current members and those they want to reach by having a culture of multiplication—exemplified by small groups—as a part of their DNA.

I hope that more and more churches see the value of expanding and multiplying groups. And I'm committed to help the church take steps in that direction as my wife and I plant a church in Mexico City. We are currently taking the first steps to launching small groups as we start our prelaunch phase. To have a reproducing and multiplying culture and healthy leaders, small groups are still the answer.

Obe Arellano serves as Latin America Catalyst for NewThing Network, coaches Spanish speaking pastors, and leads Exponential Español. Obe and his wife recently moved to Mexico City to plant a reproducing, missional church and catalyze a reproducing church movement in Latin America. Connect with Obe at ObeandJackinMexico.com.

KEY TAKEAWAYS

1. Consider a mindset toward gospel-centered multiplication not as optional, but as an essential attribute of thriving groups.
2. Remember that groups that prepare for and engage multiplication tend to be healthier than those that do not.
3. Think about and talk about multiplication regularly, and consider when your group is ready to multiply.
4. Prepare for and launch new groups with intentionality and blessing, and then ensure that you finish well.
5. When you multiply, celebrate not only what God has done in your group but the new leaders he has raised up, as well as the future impact your group will have on new groups.

REFLECTION AND DISCUSSION QUESTIONS

1. 🖐**Remember:** What caught your attention in this chapter about group multiplication?

2. 🦉**Understand:** What does multiplication mean? What are the various ways multiplication can be accomplished?

3. ⚙ **Apply:** Given the state of your current small group, how would you assess the group's readiness to multiply?

4. 🔍**Analyze:** What benefits do you foresee in multiplying your group? What challenges and/or drawbacks do you foresee?

5. 📋**Evaluate::** What reservations do you have as the group leader? In light of those reservations, how might you more readily trust in God's provision?

6. 💡 **Create:** Partner up with another leader (or two!) and develop some commitments and checkpoints for your multiplication plans.

CHAPTER 12

YOUR BEST
NEXT STEP

*Well done, good and faithful servant. You have been
faithful over a little; I will set you over much.*

—JESUS, MATTHEW 25:21

During their trip to Paris a couple of summers ago, Courtney and her husband, Matt, took a short walk to the neighborhood patisserie every morning for a delightful, flaky, authentic French croissant. A few weeks after returning home, feeling a bit "homesick" for Paris, Matt decided to try to make croissants himself. He's pretty good in the kitchen, so they were excited to see the results.

They spared no expense on the best ingredients the local grocery store had to offer. Then Matt got to work. A few hours later, with great anticipation, he pulled the croissants out of the oven. They weren't terrible, but they were dense, flat, and didn't taste the same as those they'd enjoyed every morning in Paris.

They blamed it on the ingredients. Maybe there was something about French butter that set it apart from the butter available in the US.

Determined to succeed, they decided to take a croissant-making class. They spent two and a half hours learning techniques, tips, and tricks to craft the flaky, buttery delights. Ah, it was Paris all over again. They were incredible—flaky, buttery, delicious. The

217

results were so different from what they had produced in their home kitchen. At the end of the class, Matt asked the chef where they could find the ingredients they'd used in class. Her response: "Anywhere. It's just all-purpose flour and regular unsalted butter."

They had thought it was about the ingredients. In that moment, they learned that while the quality of the ingredients is important, it's more about what you *do* with those ingredients that matters.

Throughout this book, we've laid out the recipe for thriving small groups. If you've read this far, you know the ingredients you need to develop a thriving small group. We've given you lots of tips to cultivate and develop a healthy community that contributes to individuals' spiritual growth while also taking care of yourself and expanding your influence.

REVIEW THE *LEADING SMALL GROUPS THAT THRIVE* MODEL

THE *LEADING SMALL GROUPS THAT THRIVE* MODEL

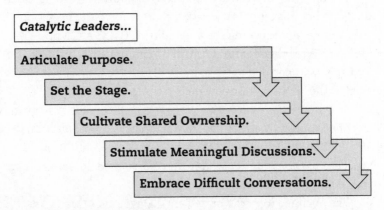

To review, catalytic leaders:

1. **Articulate Purpose.** When leaders focus on their group's unique purpose, their groups articulate and pursue a compelling purpose with fervor.
2. **Set the Stage.** When leaders set the stage by gathering the

right number of people and provide effective structures for their groups, their groups transform into spaces where devoted people pursue their unique purpose together.

3. **Cultivate Shared Ownership.** When leaders strategically invite and inspire group members to continually deepen their commitment, their members increasingly share ownership and responsibility for the group, and know and care for one another.

4. **Stimulate Meaningful Discussions.** When leaders ask great questions and facilitate good conversations, they lead their groups to experience transformational moments together.

5. **Embrace Difficult Conversations.** When leaders cultivate mutual accountability and leverage healthy tension, groups become stronger, and group members grow more mature.

TAKE YOUR BEST NEXT STEP

What are you going to do with the ingredients you've assembled? How will you skillfully and artfully put into practice the concepts and practices laid out in this book?

As Jesus says in the Parable of the Talents (Matthew 25), it's about being faithful in what God has given you. As Solomon writes in Ecclesiastes 9:10, it's about doing whatever your hand finds to do with all your might. It's about being faithful to work with what God has given you and given your group: working with diligence and care, and watching God bring the increase.

Here are five ways to identify your next best step:

If you continue leading your current group, take stock of how your group is doing. Use the Thriving Small Groups Self-Assessment, which is available at thrivinggroups.com. You might do this by yourself, or you may ask your core members to take some time to share what they see as your group's strengths and areas for growth. Then, identify 1–2 areas you think are most primed for your engagement.

Develop strategies for what you can do to help your group go to the next level. These might be big, like changing the entire structure of your group. Or they might be small, like identifying a better plan for childcare. Even small efforts and changes can reap big results.

If you plan to start a group, pursue clarity around your group's purpose in alignment with the vision for small groups we've laid out in this book. Refer back to the Purpose Development Exercise in chapter 4, and work through it (by yourself or with trusted core members of your group). Then, consider how you can develop the right size of your group to support the purpose you identify.

If you've been leading a group for a while and you feel complacency within your group, it's time to reinvigorate your group, cast a vision for multiplication, or end your group. We urge you to spend time in prayer and seek counsel from a trusted friend or your coach, pastor, or other ministry leader. Then, begin taking steps to pursue the direction you've identified.

If you feel tired, overwhelmed, or burned out as a leader, take some time to focus on self-care. Revisit chapter 9 and develop a self-care plan for the next week or month. Consider taking a group term (semester, session, or season) off in order to focus on your spiritual health. By the way, if you've raised up other leaders for your group, this might be the perfect time to allow them to occupy the space you've filled as a leader. You can step back, participate in the group, focus on self-care, and mentor your apprentice. Honestly, that might be the best thing you could offer to your group, yourself, and emerging leaders.

If you feel like you've "got this" and want to expand your influence, put your time and energy into raising up new leaders. Use the IDENTIFY → INVITE → INVEST framework shared in chapter 10. Intentionally begin to recruit and raise up leaders. If your present group doesn't give you enough opportunity, connect with your coach, pastor, or ministry leader, and offer to join their corporate leadership development efforts.

WE'RE ROOTING FOR YOU!

Leading a small group is a big deal. We're well aware that the *Leading Small Groups That Thrive* model we've laid out in these pages isn't simple. It takes lots of time. It requires a great amount of intentionality. It asks you to cultivate your skills in facilitating discussions. It says you matter. It calls you to a high standard of leadership. We wouldn't have it any other way. We don't think you would, either.

Building a healthy community is serious business, and when we do serious business, we should take stock of what it will entail. Look at what Jesus says in Luke 14:28–29:

> For which of you, desiring to build a tower, does not first sit down and count the cost, whether he has enough to complete it? Otherwise, when he has laid a foundation and is not able to finish, all who see it begin to mock him.

You've counted the cost. You know this is hard work and will require a lot of you. But you know it is worth it. You're doing this—you're leading a small group because you want to see God do incredible things in your life and in the lives of your people. You want God to do something special in those hours together. You take this seriously.

Thanks for taking this journey with us! May God grant you the strength and the wisdom to build and lead healthy communities that contribute to spiritual growth. We pray for you in line with Ephesians 3:20–21:

> God, we ask that you will do far more abundantly in these small groups and these small group leaders—now and in the future— than we could ever ask or even imagine, or that they could ever

ask or imagine. God, your power is at work in your people. Please show it, over and over again. All the glory goes to you, both now and forever!

Go, lead, and watch what God does in you and through you. We're cheering for you.

Assess and Take Action, Over and Over

Steve Gladen

Good assessments move people to action and to greater health. They don't have to be complex. They shouldn't overwhelm people. But they must be engaged continually to produce maximum effect. Throughout my twenty-plus years of leading the small groups ministry at Saddleback Church and leading the Small Group Network, I've developed two key assessments, one of which—the Spiritual Health Assessment—was used in the research for this book. I believe in the power of assessment for several reasons.

Assessments provide clarity. Too often, you don't know how your group is doing or how effective you are as a leader. Consequently, you don't know what you should do next. Assessments provide a snapshot of your group's health and effectiveness, and highlight areas of strength and weakness. After identifying what's working and what's not, you can take appropriate action. Then, when your group engages targeted exercise in identified areas, you and your group members will build spiritual and relational muscle that will strengthen you individually and collectively.

Assessments inspire short-term goal setting. By engaging regular assessment, you and your group will be urged to set goals for each season and then check progress against them.

Assessments encourage people to serve out of their strengths. Shining a light on what could be improved creates possibilities for members to step forward and meet identified needs. Just as "Necessity is often the mother of invention," identification of weak spots and associated member strengths often precedes group members stepping up into greater leadership.

Assessments make you a better leader. In *Good to Great*, leadership guru Jim Collins explained that great leaders create a climate where truth is heard and brutal facts are confronted. Your ability to identify and confront reality—what is working, what is not, what is happening, what is not—is a key step to developing your ability as a leader.

Assessments help grow healthy, thriving small groups. Over time, regularly taking stock of how your group is doing, then taking action to optimize your strengths and grow in weak areas, will stack up. Your group will build momentum, and you will experience the kind of thriving group described in this book.

For all of these reasons, make it a practice to consistently take stock of your group. Use the Purpose Development Exercise offered in this book, check out the Spiritual Health Assessment, or find another way to measure how your group is doing. As my pastor, Rick Warren, taught me many years ago, "People don't do what you expect; people do what you inspect." So inspect what you expect, and watch what God does in you and in your group through your diligence and care.

Steve Gladen is pastor of small groups at Saddleback Church in Southern California, the founder of the Small Group Network (www.smallgroupnetwork.com) and author of many small groups ministry and leadership books, including *Leading Small Groups with Purpose*. Connect at SmallGroups.net.

REFLECTION AND DISCUSSION QUESTIONS

1. 👆**Remember:** What caught your attention in this chapter?
2. 🏵️**Apply:** Which key ingredients of the *Leading Small Groups That Thrive* model are in place in your group? Which are missing?
3. 🏵️**Apply:** As you reflect on your leadership technique, what skills do you need to focus on? (If you are discussing this as part of a group of leaders, notice one another's relative areas of strength and weaknesses, and work to help each other develop them.)
4. 🔍**Analyze:** How could ongoing assessment help you grow as a leader for your group?
5. 📋**Evaluate:** What does it mean for you to be faithful in leading your small group?
6. 💡**Create:** Which of the five action steps listed in this chapter will you start with? Why?

APPENDIX A

RESOURCES TO HELP
YOU GROW AS A LEADER

Check out the *Leading Small Groups That Thrive* website at thrivinggroups.com for additional resources to help you grow into a catalytic leader, including:

1. Our list of favorite icebreakers
2. Sample group covenants
3. *Leading Small Groups That Thrive* Assessment
4. Sample group meal planning menus
5. Printable Leadership Role Strengths Assessment (from pp. 27–28)
6. Printable Purpose Development Exercise (from p. 67)
7. Printable leader's Self-Care Plan (from p. 173)

thrivinggroups.com

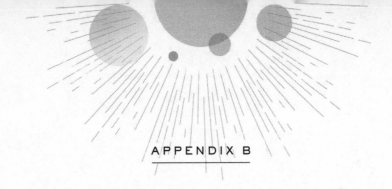

THOUGHTS AND REFLECTIVE QUESTIONS FOR PASTORS

CHAPTER 1: WHAT'S THE BIG DEAL ABOUT GROUPS?

CASTING A POWERFUL VISION FOR GROUPS

Key Insight: More than 90 percent of pastors say groups are the primary vehicle for discipleship in their church, but less than 40 percent of pastors mention groups from the pulpit on a monthly basis or more.

Questions to consider:
- Does your church have a clear vision for small groups and how they support, extend, and contribute to your church's overall discipleship strategy?
- To what extent do your leaders know the impact of small groups at your church?
- Do all of your materials—from web sign-ups, to bulletin announcements, to group leader applications, to leader training resources—share the same vision for groups at your church?

CHAPTER 2: WHAT DOES A CATALYTIC LEADER DO?

PAINTING A PICTURE OF NEXT-LEVEL GROUP LEADERSHIP

Key Insight: Because most pastors look for spiritually mature, teachable people with integrity to lead small groups, often leaders lack the skill set to actually lead a thriving group. Leadership development must be a key priority, but one-size-fits-all approaches are ineffective.

Questions to consider:
- How does your church currently develop leaders? To what extent do you provide developmental pathways that meet the needs of leaders at various stages of their development and their groups' life spans?
- Based on the *Leading Small Groups That Thrive* model, how can you expand your training systems to equip leaders with the skills they need to catalyze thriving small groups?
- How do you demonstrate the value you place on leaders? How do you talk about them, celebrate them, and show your appreciation for the key contributions they make as leaders?

CHAPTER 3: HOW DO I GET WHERE I WANT TO GO?

MAPPING A PLAN TO DEVELOP A THRIVING GROUP

Key Insight: Most groups (even work teams) take more than six months to gel, but so many small group models are built on a 10–15-week group season.

Questions to consider:
- Are you asking too much or too little from small groups based on the season model you use?
- What adjustments to your model for groups might you consider based on the insights of group development research?

- From a systems perspective, how can you enable and equip leaders to accelerate their group's growth to increase their group's chances to move to the promised land?

CHAPTER 4: CONFUSED TO COMPELLING

ENERGIZE YOUR GROUP BY ARTICULATING YOUR PURPOSE

Key Insight: Your church must be crystal-clear about why small groups exist within your discipleship and ministry framework and how they complement weekend services and other ministries and classes.

Questions to consider:
- Take a look at your stated purpose for small groups across your materials, trainings, and announcements. Does your small groups ministry benefit from a 5C (clear, compelling, challenging, calling-oriented, consistently held) purpose?
- Based on an understanding that externally focused groups contribute the most to spiritual growth, how can you shift from "creating a safe environment" or "building close relationships" in groups to pursuing the unique purpose you've identified for your ministry?
- How can you instill a clear purpose and strategy in your leadership training and ongoing communication to get everyone in your ministry speaking the same language?

CHAPTER 5: DISENGAGED TO DEDICATED

SET THE STAGE TO KEEP PEOPLE COMING BACK

Key Insight: Stimulus plus structure creates spaces where people can grow. By connecting to people's felt needs and quickly establishing predictability and relational safety, you can give your groups the soil they need to flourish.

Questions to consider:
- What are the key needs of people in your community, particularly those who are not already connected in community? How can your groups meet those important needs while still pursuing their unique purposes?
- Evaluate your sign-up mechanisms, childcare practices, policies related to using church facilities, and so on. To what extent does the suite of support you offer to small groups provide the stability and predictability new members are craving?
- What resources could be developed to help leaders more effectively manage group logistics so that people feel comfortable and ready to dive deeper into the group?

CHAPTER 6: MINE TO OURS

CULTIVATE COMMITMENT THROUGH SHARED OWNERSHIP

Key Insight: The most effective groups are owned by the entire group rather than just leaders, but the reality is that people tend to commit and invest in places where they can make a big impact, and they can only contribute significantly in a few areas of life. No one can commit with excellence to a zillion things at once.

Questions to consider:
- At your church, is there space for your leaders and group members to be all-in with their small group or are they constantly pulled in all directions? When you put it all together, what are you asking your people to do?
- Have you defined what a fully engaged group member looks like? What does the ideal group member look like?
- Considering what you ask of your leaders, are you inciting leader-only ownership? How can you help leaders move toward shared ownership?

CHAPTER 7: TRIVIAL TO TRANSFORMATIVE

STIMULATE MEANINGFUL DISCUSSIONS

Key Insight: Good leaders are not the same as good group discussion facilitators. Seeing the impact of discussion practices in contributing to spiritual growth, training leaders to facilitate discussion is a really good use of training times.

Questions to consider:
- When you write out sermon-based discussion questions, to what extent do you write good questions with discussion in mind, rather than trying to identify correct answers?
- How might you structure your weekly discussion questions based on the *Remember-Understand-Apply-Analyze-Evaluate-Create* framework?
- Have you considered developing a resource to help your leaders plan outstanding gatherings?

CHAPTER 8: AVOIDANCE TO EMBRACE

ENGAGE DIFFICULT CONVERSATIONS
WITHOUT DESTROYING YOUR GROUP

Key Insight: Leaders need to lean into tension rather than away from it, but they must have the resources to do it effectively.

Questions to consider:
- Identify some of the most challenging situations your leaders have recently experienced. How might you create case studies from those situations to train your leaders?
- To what extent do your ministry leaders talk not only about key successes related to small groups ministry, but also about the messiness and the challenging situations that didn't turn out well? Use these stories to cast a vision for and normalize challenge and tension in groups.
- What support systems are in place for when leaders engage

challenging and emotionally-taxing situations? Do they know when to consult with you? To what extent do leaders feel supported by you in times of difficulty?

CHAPTER 9: YOUR CARE

CULTIVATING AND SUSTAINING YOUR OWN HEALTH

Key Insight: Too many leaders care for others at the expense of themselves, and many coaching structures aren't built to care for the leaders as much as their leadership.

Questions to consider:
- To what extent are your leaders experiencing or approaching burnout? Do you have mechanisms in place to identify early signs of burnout in your leaders?
- How might you adapt your coaching approach with small group leaders to focus more on your leaders and their personal care in addition to their group leadership?
- What sorts of rhythms, such as sabbaticals, periodic assessment, etc., do you practice with your leaders to help them take stock of their personal health and readiness for leadership?

CHAPTER 10: YOUR LEGACY

RECRUITING AND RAISING UP NEW LEADERS

Key Insight: More availability of training prompts growth in groups. The more leaders are trained, the more their groups contribute to spiritual growth.

Questions to consider:
- Have you clearly described what constitutes leader material for your ministry? Help your leaders identify people they can guide and mentor.
- What systems do you have in place for investing in the potential new leaders that current leaders identify?

- When you look over the *Leading Small Groups That Thrive* model, in which elements do your leaders need more training and resourcing? How might you provide it to them?

CHAPTER 11: YOUR CHARGE
EXPANDING AND MULTIPLYING GROUPS

Key Insight: Groups that have multiplied and groups that are newer contribute the most to members' spiritual growth. Growth and momentum are essential to maximizing the impact groups can make.

Questions to consider:
- What is your ministry's vision for growth and expansion? To what extent have you shared your vision and your rationale with your leaders?
- How can you prepare group leaders and members for group-level multiplication thinking by encouraging them to take micro-level action, such as inviting an unchurched person to church?
- What resources do your group leaders have for:
  - Determining when to end a group
  - Ending a group gracefully
  - Launching a new group from an existing group
  - Launching a brand-new group
  - Casting a vision for continual growth

CHAPTER 12: YOUR BEST NEXT STEP

Key Insight: Continual assessment at individual leader, group, and ministry levels will enable your ministry to achieve maximum impact.

Questions to consider:
- With a few colleagues or trusted leaders, and thinking about your ministry as a whole, consider how well-equipped your group leaders are to:

- **Focus on Purpose.** Do they know and focus on their group's unique purpose under the umbrella of your ministry's overall purpose, prioritize what matters most, and continually refocus the group to pursue its purpose?
- **Set the Stage.** Following your direction and encouragement, do they pay attention to group size, gather the right people who can benefit from the group experience, structure group gatherings to support the group's purpose, and establish communication norms that set the stage for effective engagement?
- **Cultivate Shared Ownership.** Do they invite and inspire group members to continually deepen their commitment to the group by taking on greater leadership roles, spur members to share life with one another, and communicate frequently with members?
- **Stimulate Meaningful Discussions.** Are your leaders equipped to ask great questions, fully contribute themselves but let group members shine, and facilitate meaningful group discussions?
- **Embrace Difficult Conversations.** Do they stifle conflict and tension or cultivate mutual accountability and leverage healthy tension for the good of group members and the group as a whole?
- **Care for Themselves.** Do your leaders possess and act on a plan to care for themselves and continually sharpen themselves?
- **Develop Other Leaders.** Do they regularly identify potential leaders, invite them into relationship and developmental opportunities, and then invest intentionally in them?
- **Multiply and Grow.** Are your leaders regularly thinking about multiplying and taking steps—no matter the length of time their current group has been meeting—to prepare for and implement growth and multiplication practices?

Based on your answers to this quick assessment, what is the next best step for your small groups ministry?

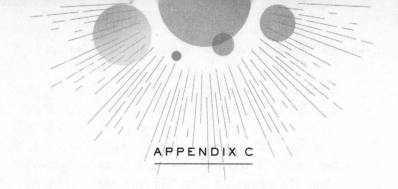

WHERE DID WE GET THESE IDEAS?

Stats, Numbers, and Data

For this mixed-method study, we employed a quantitative survey design across three populations: pastors/ministry leaders, small group leaders, and small group members.

PARTICIPANTS

We recruited small groups pastors and ministry leaders through smallgroups.com, via snowball sample, and via respondent-driven sample, enabling us to locate individuals who might also be interested in participating. Through an online survey, we invited pastors and ministry leaders to tell us about their churches—specifically, their denomination, weekly attendance figures over the last few years, and geographic location. We also asked them about their specific small groups ministry models—what their primary purposes are, what they look for in leaders, how they train their leaders, how they organize groups, and how involved their members are in groups.

We then asked them to nominate 3–5 of their best current small groups—at least one group among their very best and at least two groups they considered to be "above average." From there, and with the encouragement of those pastors, we invited leaders and members from those nominated groups to tell us about their small groups. We asked them about their individual spiritual health and growth, how they spent their group time, communication between leaders and members, discussion practices and experiences with other group members.

In total, 90 small groups pastors and ministry leaders participated, which then yielded a sample of 135 leaders and 825 members of "above average" small groups, as nominated by their pastors or ministry leaders.

The pastor/ministry leader data represented churches ranging in weekly attendance from 30 to 3900 ($M = 1158$, $SD = 1075$) and reported on average 48 percent church participation in small groups. With regard to church denomination, 39 percent of our sample identified as non-denominational, 11 percent identified as Baptist (SBC, ABC, other), and 8 percent identified as Assemblies of God/Pentecostal/ Foursquare. The Christian & Missionary Alliance, Christian Church, Evangelical Free, Friends/Quaker, Methodist, Nazarene, and Presbyterian/Reformed denominations are also represented in the sample. Additionally, the sample comprised churches from over twenty-two states in the US and three churches abroad.

The leaders and members ranged in age from nineteen to eighty-three years ($M = 44.5$, $SD = 14.1$), and 36 percent of the sample identified as male. Eighty-seven percent of the sample identified as White, 5.6 percent Hispanic, 4.3 percent Asian/Pacific Islander, 3.4 percent Black, and 1.3 percent American Indian. Participants had attended their respective churches from two months to forty-six years ($M = 8.5$ years, $SD = 7.9$ years).

MEASURES

Our key outcome variable was adapted from Steve Gladen's Spiritual Health Assessment, measuring individual spiritual health.[1] In addition to attitudinal measures, each dimension was augmented by a behavioral measure, asking about frequency of concrete behaviors. The items, some of which were reverse-coded, are as follows:

WORSHIP: YOU WERE PLANNED FOR GOD'S PLEASURE

1. I desire to please and honor Jesus in all that I do.
2. If I go several days without reading the Bible, I find myself unfulfilled.
3. How I live my life shows that God is my highest priority.
4. About how often, if at all, do you personally read the Bible (not including church worship services, small group, or other church-sponsored event)?

FELLOWSHIP: YOU WERE FORMED FOR GOD'S FAMILY

1. I have a deep and meaningful connection with others in the church.
2. I do not gather regularly with a group of Christians for fellowship and accountability.
3. I intentionally spend time with other believers (outside of my spouse/family) in order to help them grow in their faith.
4. In a typical month, about how many times (if any) do you gather with other adults from church outside of church-sponsored activities?

DISCIPLESHIP: YOU WERE CREATED TO BECOME LIKE CHRIST

1. A review of how I use my finances shows that I think more about God and others than I do about myself.
2. I feel sorrow and regret when I realize I have sinned.
3. When I realize my attitude does not please God, I take steps to try and fix it.
4. About how often, if at all, do you meet with at least one other believer (excluding spouses and roommates) for discipleship purposes (e.g., confess your sins to others, pray, read the Bible together, share or seek biblical advice)?

MINISTRY: YOU WERE SHAPED FOR SERVING GOD

1. I am currently serving God with the gifts and passions he has given me.

2. I am intentionally putting my spiritual gift(s) to use serving God and others.
3. I intentionally try to serve people outside my church who have tangible needs.
4. About how often, if at all, do you find yourself meeting a perceived need without being asked?

EVANGELISM: YOU WERE MADE FOR A MISSION

1. While interacting with others on a normal, daily basis, I seek opportunities to speak out about Jesus Christ.
2. My heart is full of passion to share the good news of the gospel with those who have never heard it.
3. I find that my relationship with Jesus comes up frequently in my conversations with those who do not know him.
4. In the past six months, about how many times have you personally invited an unchurched person to attend a church service, small group, or other church-sponsored event or activity?

Additionally, we asked about the extent to which their current small group contributed to each of the above-mentioned dimensions of spiritual health.

We also assessed a variety of group practices:

- **Time.** We asked about how much time the group spent together during each regularly scheduled group meeting and how that time was spent (e.g., fellowship, discussion/study, serving others, prayer, worship, logistics/announcements).
- **Group discussion.** We learned about group members' willingness to say hard things and the extent to which they talk among themselves as opposed to talking to the leader and the leader talking back to them individually. We asked about group rules, accountability, and leaders' willingness to confront group members about contributing to the group.

- **Group conflict.** We asked about the existence of conflict and the leader's role in facilitating conflict management.
- **Biblical community.** We asked about connecting with other members and the extent to which members had shared their story with other members and how many others' stories they knew.
- **Leader characteristics.** We asked members to assess the credibility of their leaders: their expertise, trustworthiness, and goodwill.
- **Communication frequency and leader commitment.** We asked members to share how frequently their leader(s) communicated with them as a behavioral measure of their commitment to the group and its members.
- **Group gatherings.** We asked about the kinds of questions leaders ask during group gatherings and how they lead and facilitate discussions.

Separately, we asked leaders:

- **Their small group priorities.** Using Gladen's five dimensions, we asked leaders about the priorities of their specific small groups.
- **Leader development.** We asked how they have been developed as leaders and their previous group leadership experience.
- **Group membership demographics.** They reported the number of members in the group, the percentage of members who attended 75 percent and 50 percent of the time, and how long the group had been together.
- **Commitment to the group.** We measured commitment by asking leaders how committed they were.
- **Multiplication.** We asked if the group had multiplied, and if so, how many times, how often, and how many individuals and couples had left the group to serve as leaders of a new group.

DATA ANALYSIS

When we asked members to share how much their small group contributed to each of the above-mentioned dimensions of their spiritual health, we computed the average for each individual (Cronbach's alpha = .854, indicating a strong measure of the five items comprising the small group's contribution to one's spiritual health). For each group, the average scores of each member were then averaged to provide a group-level average. Thus, the average of how much each member reported that the group contributed to his or her individual spiritual health became our primary, group-level, dependent variable, while controlling for the spiritual health of each individual in the group in each of our statistical tests.

We conducted rigorous data analysis, including multiple regression and ANOVAs, to assess relationships among variables. From this data, only statistically significant results were presented. Additionally, we identified the small groups that had the highest scores on our dependent variable, the group's contribution to their individuals' spiritual health. Several of the top twenty groups were also profiled in our data.

We also followed up with site visits and interviews with several of the top 20 groups, observing and asking questions about their particular group practices. We collected stories from group leaders to learn about their groups' experiences, challenges, success stories, and practices.

This book and the recommendations throughout represent this rich set of data, supported by additional psychological and communication research, presented to help leaders facilitate individual spiritual growth through small group practices.

ACKNOWLEDGMENTS

Many more than three names should be on the cover of this book. Truly, this book is only possible because of the generous investments of time, energy, and insights from so many friends, colleagues, and strangers.

We're most grateful to the triune God who said, "Let us make man in our image" (Gen. 1:26), modeling for us from the very beginning of time the great joy of intimate small group fellowship, and creating us to crave the same. It is this incredible God whom we follow, not just in how we worship and live but also in how we thrive in community.

To the nearly 1,000 small group members, leaders, and pastors who helped us to learn what is working and what isn't in their groups and small groups ministries, we're so grateful. Thank you for letting us learn from you. We earnestly hope we've been able to capture what we've learned from you in a way that benefits the cause of discipleship now and into eternity.

We're also grateful for all those who read and suggested improvements on early drafts of this book and who supported us early on as we got the project going: Brad Himes, Ike Graham, Katie DuBransky, David Fletcher, Heidi Ross, DJ Smith, Abigail Wong, Amy Jackson, Larry Osborne, Warren Bird, and, of course, our spouses, Jill Hartwig, Nicole Sniff, and Matt Davis. Each of you certainly made this book much better. Special shout-outs go to Amy Jackson and Rob Toal of *Christianity Today*'s smallgroups.com, who helped us launch our research project, and Steve Gladen, who graciously allowed us to use his framework for assessing group spiritual health. Thank you so much.

Each of us enjoys a special system of support where we work. We acknowledge the research grant by the Faculty Research Council at Azusa Pacific University, which enabled the data collection and analysis of this project, as well as many colleagues at Colorado Christian University, Azusa Pacific University, and Eastview Christian Church who have made it possible for us to pursue this research. Special thanks to Dr. David Dunaetz, who assisted with our quantitative data analysis, and four fantastic students—Anna Dickinson, Sierra Bridge, Samie True, and Christina Kasali—who managed the research project, helped with qualitative data analysis, and provided editorial and marketing support throughout the project.

We deeply appreciate the support, guidance, and coaching offered by the editorial and marketing team at Zondervan: Ryan Pazdur, Liz Vince, Harmony Harkema, and Nathan Kroeze. You've kindly put up with our many revisions and requests, and it has been a joy to work with such a fantastic team of professionals.

Finally, we couldn't do this without the support of the ones we love and who love us so well.

Ryan says: Jill, you're the greatest gift I've ever been given (other than eternal life)! I'm so grateful we get to journey through this life together. Halle, Alia, Kate, and Matt, being your dad is the greatest honor of my life. Thanks for all your love and support on this project—the grace when I'm away, the cookies to keep me fueled, and the hugs and wrestling matches that root me. I love you! To all of those who have blessed me by getting to walk through a portion of life with you in a small group, thank you for lovingly investing in my life. You inspired this work. Last, thanks to my family, friends, and mentors who have dreamed with me, sacrificed for me, and poured into me. Everything I've learned is because of your generosity to me.

Courtney says: Matt, your sacrificial leadership in our marriage and family has propelled me to so many good yeses in our life like this opportunity. Luke and Theo, what a joy it is (most days!) to be your mom. You three make up the most important small group of which I will ever be a part, and because of you, I am becoming more of who God is creating me to be. And to the members of the many other small groups of which I have been a part, including my family, friends, sorority, churches, and workplaces, and especially to our Wednesday night growth group, which has encouraged me through this book-writing process, thank you for your role in spurring me on toward love and good deeds in the last twenty years. I am grateful to God for each of you.

Jason says: Nicole, you inspired and encouraged me to keep going when this endeavor seemed too much. Thank you for always believing in me and walking hand in hand as we journey this life together. Team Sniff (Damion, KJ, Drake, Lucas, Hanna Joy, and Jennavieve), you bring so much life and light. We might be crazy and living on the edge of Normal (IL), but I wouldn't change it for anything. Eastview Christian Church, thank you for being a safe place where my family has grown up and chosen to follow Jesus and a place genuinely dedicated to loving people wholeheartedly for Jesus. Your care and support for me and Team Sniff has been invaluable. Finally, Grammy and Grandpa, and Amma and Pappa, your support while I traveled and wrote was priceless.

NOTES

INTRODUCTION: WHY WE NEEDED THIS BOOK (AND WHY YOU MIGHT ALSO)

1. Steve Gladen, *Small Groups with Purpose* (Grand Rapids, MI: Baker Books, 2011).
2. To learn more about our research approach, see appendix C.

CHAPTER 1: WHAT'S THE BIG DEAL ABOUT GROUPS?

1. Ed Stetzer and Eric Geiger, *Transformational Groups* (Nashville: B&H, 2014), 198.
2. For instance, Nelson Searcy's "Activate" small group system is built on the principle that groups are not a place where intimate friendships are formed, but where new friendships are formed. However, every church/ministry should evaluate the best role that small groups should play in their ministry, including whether that is deep or introductory friendship.
3. See also Jim Davis, "5 Reasons We Switched from Small Groups to Sunday School," The Gospel Coalition, Nov. 30, 2017, https://www .thegospelcoalition.org/article/5-reasons-we-switched-from-small -groups-to-sunday-school/. However, the principles laid out in this book apply to all kinds of groups gathering for various purposes and in various formats, including classes. We do not advocate for any particular structure/model of small groups, yet recognize there is no way to do "church" without forming people into some kind of group where they grow together spiritually.
4. Jennifer A. Guthrie and Adrienne Kunkel, "Communication in Support Groups," *The International Encyclopedia of Interpersonal Communication* (Hoboken: John Wiley & Sons, Inc, 2016).
5. Susan. R Suleiman, "Introduction" in *Exile and Creativity: Signposts, Travelers, Outsiders, Backward Glances.* S. R. Suleiman, Ed. (Durham, NC: Duke University Press, 1996), 1.

6. For a great resource on how to practice biblical hospitality with evangelistic vision, see *The Simplest Way to Change the World* by Dustin Willis and Brandon Clements (Chicago: Moody Publishers, 2017).
7. Mark Howell, "10 Assumptions that Shape My Small Group Ministry Strategy," Mark Howell Live, http://www.markhowelllive.com/10-assumptions-that-shape-my-small-group-ministry-strategy/.
8. Many of the names used in this book are pseudonyms, but they are all real stories of small group leaders and members we interacted with or heard about from others.

CHAPTER 2: WHAT DOES A CATALYTIC LEADER DO?

1. James R. Meindl,. Sanford B. Ehrlich, and. Janet M. Dukerich, "The Romance of Leadership" *Administrative Science Quarterly* vol. 30, no. 1 (March, 1985): 87–102.
2. See, for instance, J. Richard Hackman J. R., and Ruth Wageman, "When and How Team Leaders Matter," *Research in Organizational Behavior*, vol. 26 (2005), 37–74.
3. Remember, we frame "effectiveness" as the extent to which a group experience positively contributes to the spiritual growth of the members of a group, and not just the spiritual health of members.
4. Jim Egli, "Quit Being a Cry-Baby Groups Pastor and Focus on the 2 Key Things That Produce Results," Jim Egli (blog), Nov. 29, 2013, http://jimegli.com/quit-being-a-cry-baby-group-pastor-focus-on-the-2-things-that-produce-results/.
5. Surratt, Chris. *Leading Small Groups* (Nashville, TN: B&H Publishing, 2019), 12–13.
6. This was one of Willow Creek's five core assumptions, embedded in their small group ministry strategy in the 1990s.

CHAPTER 3: HOW DO I GET WHERE I WANT TO GO?

1. Susan Wheelan, *Creating Effective Teams: A Guide for Members and Leaders*, 5th ed. (Thousand Oaks, CA: Sage Publications, Inc., 2016), 24–30.
2. Wheelan, 133–134.

CHAPTER 4: CONFUSED TO COMPELLING

1. All names of churches (and their members) are fictitious, unless the church specifically gave us permission to use its actual name.
2. Ed Stetzer and Eric Geiger, *Transformational Groups* (Nashville, TN: B&H Publishing Company, 2014), 21.
3. For more discussion on this principle, see *Transformational Groups*, chapter 4 (Stetzer & Geiger, 2014).

4. See guest commentary by Dave Ferguson at the end of this chapter for an example of what this looks like.

5. Jon Katzenbach and Doug Smith, *The Wisdom of Teams: Creating the High-Performance Organization* (New York: Harper Business, 1999), 49.

6. Donald Miller, *A Million Miles in a Thousand Years* (Nashville: Thomas Nelson, 2009).

7. Chris Surratt, *Small Groups for the Rest of Us* (Nashville, TN: Thomas Nelson, 2015), 7.

8. See Nelson Searcy's *Activate* for more discussion about this concept.

9. For a great discussion on determining your group's purpose within a larger church/ministry, especially for pastors and ministry leaders, see chapter 4 of *Transformational Groups* (Stetzer and Geiger, 2014).

10. Stetzer and Geiger, *Transformational Groups*.

CHAPTER 5: DISENGAGED TO DEDICATED

1. Richard Thaler and Cass Sunstein, *Nudge: Improving Decisions about Health, Wealth, and Happiness* (New York Penguin Books, 2009), 8.

2. Larry Osborne, *Sticky Church* (Grand Rapids, MI: Zondervan, 2008), 79.

3. Bill Search, *The Essential Guide for Small Group Leaders* (Carol Stream, IL: Christianity Today, 2017), 19–20.

4. Greg Ogden, *Transforming Discipleship* (Downers Grove, IL: InterVarsity Press, 2016), 55.

5. For more about comparing the pros and cons of different kinds of spaces, see Parker's *The Art of Gathering*.

6. See, for instance, Jill Suttie, "How Music Bonds Us Together," *Greater Good Magazine*, June 28, 2016, https://greatergood.berkeley.edu/article /item/how_music_bonds_us_together.

7. To further explore how you can prepare and prime your guests to contribute right off the bat, see Parker's *The Art of Gathering* (London, UK: Penguin Books, 2019).

8. To ensure safety and compliance with legal requirements related to a church/ministry paying childcare staff, be sure to check with your pastor or ministry leader about the requirements for proper vetting and background checks, and so on.

CHAPTER 6: MINE TO OURS

1. Want to know the rest of the story? Aaron is one of John's best friends to this day. About nine months after that awkward conversation, Aaron's wife returned home. They're going strong and recently baptized their two kids!

2. Henri Nouwen, *In the Name of Jesus* (New York: Chestnut Ridge, 1997), 43.

CHAPTER 7: TRIVIAL TO TRANSFORMATIVE

1. Alex Pentland, "The New Science of Building Great Teams," *Harvard Business Review*, April 2012, https://hbr.org/2012/04/the-new-science -of-building-great-teams.
2. Steve Gladen, *Leading Small Groups with Purpose* (Grand Rapids, MI: Baker Books, 2011), 47.
3. Lorin W. Anderson, David R. Krathwohl, and Benjamin Samuel Bloom, *A Taxonomy for Learning, Teaching, and Assessing: A Revision of Bloom's Taxonomy of Educational Objectives* (London, United Kingdom: Longman, 2001).
4. Mark L. Knapp and Judith A. Hall, *Nonverbal Communication in Human Interaction* (NY: Harcourt Brace Jovanovich, 2002), 369.
5. Patricia Raybon, *My First White Friend: Confessions on Race, Love and Forgiveness* (New York: Penguin, 1997), 208.

CHAPTER 8: AVOIDANCE TO EMBRACE

1. Peter Scazzero, *Emotionally Healthy Spirituality* (Grand Rapids, MI: Zondervan, 2017), 48.

CHAPTER 9: YOUR CARE

1. G. C. Morgan, *Exposition of the Whole Bible* (Eugene, OR: Wipf and Stock Publishers, 2010), 41.
2. Dr. Henry Cloud, *Necessary Endings: The Employees, Businesses, and Relationships That All of Us Have to Give Up in Order to Move Forward* (New York: HarperBusiness, 2010), 7.
3. Dann Spader, *4 Chair Discipling* (Chicago, IL: Moody Publishers, 2014), 113.
4. Personal conversation with J.K. Jones, pastor, professor, author, and spiritual formation enthusiast.
5. Joseph Joubert, *Joubert: A Selection from His Thoughts,* Katharine Lyttelton, trans. (New York: Dodd, Mead & Co., 1899), XVIII.
6. Jim Egli, "4 Surprising Discoveries about Small Group Growth," Jim Egli (blog), Aug. 24, 2013, *jimegli.com/4-surprising-discoveries-about-small -group-growth/.*
7. Egli, "4 Surprising Discoveries about Small Group Growth."
8. Egli., "4 Surprising Discoveries about Small Group Growth."
9. Carey Nieuwhof, "Dear Discouraged Leader," Carey Nieuwhof (blog), https://careynieuwhof.com/dear-discouraged-leader-5-questions -to-ask-before-you-implode/.

CHAPTER 10: YOUR LEGACY

1. Dave Ferguson and Warren Bird, *Hero Maker* (Grand Rapids: Zondervan, 2018), 64

2. Ibid.

3. *Hero Maker* is a great resource for identifying and raising up leaders in the church.

4. For more information about the different theological perspectives on women in leadership and how these perspectives play out in everyday ministry, download Kadi's free Theological Cheat Sheet at www.KadiCole.com/Resources.

CHAPTER 11: YOUR CHARGE

1. For more nuggets from Tom Peters, visit https://www.toolshero.com /toolsheroes/tom-peters/.

2. Joel Comiskey, *Cell-Based Ministry: A Positive Factor for Church Growth in Latin America* (dissertation, Fuller Theological Seminary, 1997), 261, https://joelcomiskeygroup.com/wp-content/uploads/2017/10 /comiskeyDissertation.pdf.

3. Bob McNabb, *Spiritual Multiplication in the Real World* (Multiplication Press, 2013), 71.

APPENDIX C: WHERE DID WE GET THESE IDEAS? STATS, NUMBERS, AND DATA

1. Steve Gladen, *Small Groups with Purpose* (Grand Rapids, MI: Baker Books, 2011).